Essays on Indian Historiography

Essays on
Indian Historiography

H.A. Phadke

RAWAT PUBLICATIONS
Jaipur • New Delhi • Bangalore • Mumbai

ISBN 81-7033-925-1

Published by
Prem Rawat for *Rawat Publications*
Satyam Apts., Sector 3, Jawahar Nagar, Jaipur 302 004 (India)
Phone: 0141 265 1748 / 7006 Fax: 0141 265 1748
E-mail: info@rawatbooks.com
Website: www.rawatbooks.com

Delhi Office
4858/24, Ansari Road, Daryaganj, New Delhi 110 002
Phone: 011-23263290

Also at Bangalore and Mumbai

Typeset by Rawat Computers, Jaipur
Printed at Chaman Enterprises, New Delhi

Pitarau Vande

Dedicated
to
the Sacred Memory
of
Pt. Anant Shastri Phadke, my father
and
Shri D.K. Godbole, my father-in-law

Contents

II
Social and Intellectual Movements in Maharashtra (Nineteenth Century)

Preface

This is a modest attempt at exposing some basic problems of Indian historiography which have tremendously influenced our cultural, social, intellectual and political life in modern times.

The opening chapter investigates into what could be the central philosophy of the Gita and what is its relevance today? It has been pointed out that Karmayoga received due attention only during the modern period because of the development of scientific attitude towards the understanding of human activities. The following chapter ascertains Vyasa's position as the founder of Indian historical tradition with special reference to his contribution to the development of Bhagavata religion, Purana Pravakta, the author of the Brahmasutras and the Bharat Savitri and finally, his claims to the remembrance of history. The third chapter discusses the problem of dating early Indian history with specific reference to the date of the Bharata Battle and the beginning of the traditional Kaliyuga and has well refuted the Yugabda 5101 theory of dating Indian history as propagated by the Bharatiya Itihasa Samkalana Samiti.

'Sati' and 'Ayodhya' are subjects of wider national concern. A historiographical analysis of the sources is essential before inferences are drawn. The idealistic view of life, the impact of tradition on popular and to some extent on educated minds and its reaction to any constructive approach to social change have been thoroughly probed.

In our historical thinking Panjab occupies a special position. It has been the centre of early civilisations and culture and a guardian as it were, of the security and stability of the Indo-Gangetic plains. This unique geopolitical situation of the region depends on its material conditions which have also determined its socio-economic and cultural formations. This has been brought out in the sixth and seventh chapters.

'National Integration' and 'Nehru's Rationalism' are themes of perennial significance and relevance. Integration, no more a problem of national concern only, has assumed global relevance. As says J. Krishnamurty, "it is neither the action of will nor it is the process of being integrated. It is a state of complete attention." And the totality of Nehru's life-work based on his scientific humanism ever remains a subject of historical speculation.

The impact of the West and the growth of intellectual movement has drawn considerable attention of scholars in modern times. In Western India, it was marked by reforms in socio-religious, educational and judicial spheres and specially it can be observed in the growth of Indological consciousness.

The studies are based on a variety of sources, archaeological data, Brahmanical, Buddhist, Jaina and Puranic literature, the observations of classical writers – Greek, Roman, Chinese, Persian – archival material and Marathi records besides various research journals, all have been fully made use of.

I offer my grateful thanks to my esteemed friend the late Pt. Setumadhavrao Pagadi of Bombay, for his blessings and valuable suggestions on points concerning historical developments in Western India. My thanks are also due to the librarians of Kurukshetra University, Kurukshetra and Mumbai Marathi Granth Samgrahalaya, Dadar, Bombay for their kind help in providing invaluable source material.

Hari Anant Phadke

Acknowledgements

We are thankful to the editors and publishers of the volumes wherein the essays have been published before. These are: Proceedings of the Punjab History Conference, Panjabi University, Patiala, 1988; The Sources of the History of India, Vol. V, Institute of Historical Studies, Calcutta, 1984; Proceedings of the Seminar on Ayodhya: History, Archaeology and Tradition, Kashiraj Trust, Varanasi, 1995; Proceedings of the National Seminar on Sati, Banaras Hindu University, Varanasi, 1989; Vishvambhara, Harman Publishing House, New Delhi, 1995; Haryana Review, Chandigarh, 1981; Proceedings of the Indian History Congress, Dharwad Session, 1988; Journal of Ancient Indian History, Calcutta University, 1991; Ratnachandrika, Harman Publishing House, New Delhi, 1989 and Proceedings of the Regional Seminar on Socio-economic History, March, 1991, Kurukshetra University, Nos. 1 and 11 are recent additions and have not been published so far.

I

Cultural, Social and Political

1

Srimadbhagavadgita: The Historical View

Srimadbhagavadgita, incorporated in the Bhishmaparva of the Mahabharata, was not really a sudden isolated creation. It had behind it centuries of deep meditation and speculation nurtured since the Vedas, the Brahmanas and the Upanishadas, reaching its culmination at Dharmakshetra Kurukshetra. The reference to the Gita as Upanishad, Brahmavidya (the science of the absolute) and Yogashastra (the scripture of yoga) in the usual colophon appearing at the end of every *adhyaya* (chapter) of the text would justify the statement made at the very outset. The studies on the Gita in modern times, both by Western and Indian scholars, are concerned mainly with such aspects as the indebtedness of the text to earlier currents of Indian philosophical thought,[1] tracing its antiquity, coming as it were in reaction to the powerful tendency among some of the eminent Western scholars, to find in Christ a prototype of Krishna and in the Bible the origin of the Gita and believing our Puranic literature to be a merely later growth;[2] or intensely discussing the claims of each of its three fundamental concepts, viz., Jnana (knowledge), Bhakti (devotion) and Karma (action) for being the central theme of the text. The first and the second aspects of the subject are also reflected in the treatises of the Acharyas on the Gita[3] in early periods of our history and in the compositions of the poets of the Bhakti school during the medieval period.[4]

The Gita is called an Upanishad because it derives its main inspiration from that remarkable group of scriptures called the Upanishadas. The *Vaishnaviya Tantrasara*, in one of its popular verses, makes out that the Gita "restates the central teachings of the Upanishadas."[5] Textual analysis has revealed that the Gita was written later than the early Upanishadas (*c.* 700 – 500 B.C.) and approximately it coincides in time with the so-called middle Upanishadas (*c.* 200 B.C. – 400 A.D.). This continuity is reflected not only in the similarity relating to many principles of doctrine and in the use of identical terms but also in direct, almost word-for-word coincidences.[6]

The Gita is mainly concerned with the full exposition of the ways (marga), i.e., Jnana (knowledge), Bhakti (devotion) and Karma (action) leading the faithfuls to the supreme goal of liberation (*moksha*). However, there are no unequivocal indications as to which of the three is the most important. The text is also not of any help in determining the original strata which belonged to the Bharata battle and which provided the occasion for the development of a spiritual message based on ancient wisdom (*prajna purani*) of the Upanishadas. Nevertheless, it can be reasonably guessed that the devastating results of a war, physical, moral and spiritual, as portrayed by Arjuna in the opening chapter of the Gita, are not just an imagery but are based on the author's keen observation and knowledge of facts gathered from early historical tradition.[7]

Although in its exposition of the Jnana-yoga the Gita closely follows the Upanishadas, its concept of Karma-yoga is something absolutely original. It is precisely the proposition relating to the 'way of disinterested action' that provides the work the basic theme which distinguishes the Gita from other Indian schools of religious and philosophical thought proclaiming *moksha* as the single goal of human existence. Should man live in the world or renounce it? The Gita provides an exceedingly simple answer to the questions. "Action ceases to be a fetter when it is undertaken in a disinterested way, in such a state of mind where there is no longer any thought of acquisition to be achieved through action."[8] In its elaboration of the ideal of liberation for the individual from the bounds of worldly life as exposed in the Upanishadas, the Gita provides completely different conceptual expression of that ideal. The text of the poem is essentially devoted to an elucidation of this central idea. This has been thoroughly exposed in B.G. Tilak's *Gitarahasya* or *Karmayogashastra*[9] which interpretation has been largely acknowledged by both eastern and western scholars, but of course, with some difference in matters of interpretation.[10]

Thus, the action which the Gita recommends for the betterment of humanity has to be undertaken in a spirit of complete detachment and without any concern for the results. Its stress on contemplation, its metaphysical character and sublimity of profound thinking makes it both simple and philosophical. And its synthesis of the three ways of self-realisation (viz., yoga of Jnana, Bhakti and Karma) is simply unique. The fundamental question concerning the purpose of existence which the Gita so brilliantly poses and answers makes it exceptionally universal. Probably, there is no work in the literature of mankind where such high and profound philosophy beautifully harmonises with the simple religious precepts.[11]

The Gita is called *Brahmavidya* or the science of the absolute. It is synonymous with the term *Madhuvidya* appearing in some of the Rigvedic hymns, in the Brahmanas and the Upanishadas wherein questions regarding ultimate reality (Brahma) and its relation with individual soul (Atman), the origin of universe and manifestations of nature, in intelligible and beautiful forms were raised and partly answered.[12] To help us to understand, the nature of reality is the purpose of Brahmavidya, for logical investigation is of great help in the acquisition of spiritual wisdom. Shankara, in the *Aparokshanubhuti*, observes that "without inquiry, wisdom cannot be attained by any other means, even as things of the world cannot be seen without light".[13]

The Gita is also designated as *Yogashastra* or the art of union with reality. Philosophy is very much related to life for 'action begins only where the thought ends". As observed by Radhakrishnan:[14]

> Marx's criticism that philosophers interpret the world while the real task is to change it does not apply to the author of the Gita who gave us not only a philosophical interpretation, Brahmavidya but also a practical programme, Yogashastra. Our world is not a spectacle to contemplate, it is a field of battle. Only for the Gita improvement in the individual nature is the way to social betterment.

It may be noted that J. Krishnamurti does not differ essentially with the above interpretation while asserting that "fundamental change in society cannot be brought without the inner transformation of the individual".[15] The teaching of the Gita thus corresponds with the religions of mankind. It represents "not merely Hinduism but religion as such, in its universality, without limit of time and space"[16] and hence, as very beautifully put by Aldous Huxley "*its enduring value, not only for Indians, but for all mankind ..... The Bhagavadgita is perhaps the most systematic spiritual statement of the Perennial Philosophy*".[17] The meaning of existence as explained by the Gita provides the basis "for agreement in mind and spirit so very essential for keeping together the world which has become materially one by the universal acceptance of externals of civilisation".[18]

The theory of action may seem to be the focal point of the philosophy and ethics of the Gita but it remarkably harmonises with earlier phases of spiritual thought bringing them all into an integrated system, 'free and large, subtle and profound'. The unity of God, matter and spirit – the twin aspects of the one, the absolute, and the cult of sacrifice as exposed in the Vedic literature, the Upanishadic teaching of the transcendent Brahman, the Bhagavata theism and 'tender piety', the Saṁkhya dualism and the Yoga meditation, all these elements are brought into 'an organic unity'. The method is "not of denial but of penetration showing how these different lines of thought converge towards the same end".[19]

The exposition of the true nature of action, both good and evil, seems to be the main purpose of the Gita. This is in agreement with its modern commentators Tilak, Aurobindo, Vivekanand, Gandhi, Vinoba, Radhakrishnan, Hiriyanna and others.[20] The theory of action (*Karmamarga*) is in a better position for claims to be regarded as the central theme of the Gita. The proposition may also be historically viable for whatever may be the chronological position of the composition of the Gita, it is invariably associated with the historical personages belonging to the close of the Rigvedic and the beginning of the later-Vedic period.[21] This was also the period when the Bharatas were dominant over the Indo-Gangetic plains. The battle which presented the occasion for raising fundamental question regarding the meaning of existence was a concern mainly of the Bharata tribes which justifies the title of the great epic – the Mahabharata.

The society then was tribal, semi-pastoral and agricultural. Assimilation of the Vedic and non-Vedic had already started and with the merger of several Vedic tribes among themselves, Bharata-Puru and the Kuru for instance, ground was prepared for the formation of territorial states in the subsequent period. Rigid caste and occupational groupings were not yet formed. The perpetual occupational groupings had turned war into 'a natural economic function' and pastoralism brought patriarchal element to the fore and relegated women to lower position. The unequal sharing of wealth further led to the emergence of the institution of kingship. What contents of the Gita, it may be asked, could be reconciled with this social formation which belongs to the period of Bharata-Puru-Kuru tribal assimilation as indicated above and which was later on joined by the Panchalas?[22]

The assimilation of these tribes took place due to the conquest of one people by another and this process, whereby tribes were transformed into peoples and nations, was a common feature during the Vedic period. That the Panchalas joined the Kurus finds support in their frequent mention along with the Kurus in the later-Vedic period. The Kurus were thus the most prominent people of that period. It may also be remembered that the country received its name Bharata after the Bharatas while the Kurus founded Kurukshetra and determined its religious character.[23] It was again at Kurukshetra (earlier called Sharyanavat) that the Rigvedic *Madhuvidya* or *Brahmavidya* was formulated, and the Brahmanas which are next in importance only to the Samhitas were composed.[24] Thus associated with Vedic compositions and their recitation, and the performance of the *yajnas*, this region set forth model for purity of speech and its standards of piety and conduct were considered (subsequently) worthy of emulation "by the entire humanity all over the world".[25] This explains why Kurukshetra was chosen as a befitting place for the battle of the Mahabharata, and why the message of the Bhagvadgita was delivered here. The title of the great epic reveals, quite significantly, the Bharata connections of the contending parties. This besides, in the Gita, Arjuna is addressed as Bharata, Bharatarshabha, Bharatashreshtha, Bharatasattama and also Kurunandana, Kurushreshta, Kurusattama and Kurupravira. In fact, the Pandavas after their victory in the war, succeeded to the Kuru realm as Kurus.[26] In the making of Kurukshetra as a seat of religion and culture the Kurus made a distinct contribution by performing sacrifices, by their spirit of religious devotion and idealism and by their innate literary and spiritual resources and last but not the least, their excellence in military skill.[27] They were remembered as authorities on the whole corpus of Vedic ritualism while their moral code of conduct and superiority in spiritual matters were considered for special commendations even during the times of Buddha and thereafter.[28]

From the above it would appear that Kurukshetra had been a traditional seat of spiritual learning and a field of tribal conflicts before the Bharata battle which provided the theme to the composer of the Bhagavadgita. The credit for this elevation of the place goes to its founders – the Kurus whose life-story particularly their contributions to Indian spiritual thought, need to be taken into account for any serious investigation into the genesis and growth of the thought contents or the Gita. So far scholars have depended exclusively on the internal evidence gathered from textual criticism, its comparison with ideas in the texts belonging to the various schools of Indian philosophy in order to establish its antiquity. In this process attempts were also made to identify the original, among the three main concepts of the Gita, namely, Jnana, Bhakti and Karma. Of the three the way of Karma may be said to have been anticipated by the Rigvedic seers in their emphasis on Rita or the moral order which comes closer to the idea of Dharma as conceived in Indian thought.[29]

According to the Mahabharata unlawful usurpation of land was the main cause of the war. It was believed that he "who owns land, owns all". In its most simple form, the issue related to dispute about the land involving family honour and virtue, which were threatened by men who prided themselves in their self-righteousness. But this dispute ostensibly of a mundane nature finally assumes the character of the law of good and evil (*Karyakaryavyavasthiti*)[30] which forms indeed the very core of Tilak's *Karmayogashastra* or *Gitarahasya*.[31] The contributions of Vishvamitra, Vasistha, Vamadeva and the Brigus, the eminent priests of the kings of the Bharata-Puru line to the development of Indian spiritual thought and that of the Kuru-Panchalas of the Brahmanic and Upanishadic fame, the *Ashtangamahadharma* of King Kuru, the excellence of Devapi in ritualistic matters and the masterly exposition of Bhishma on religion, ethics and polity and last but not the least, Vyasa

Parasarya, the founder of Indian historical tradition, all need to be properly considered while discussing the original strata of the thought-content of the Gita. Further, the Kuru-Dharma and Shila of the Buddhist texts and the special mention of Yudhishthira, Dhananjaya and Vidura Pandit in the Jatakas[32] and the relationship between Bhagavadgita and Mahayanism[33] also need to be explained. The sociological and cultural aspects involved in the proposed study would certainly put it in proper historical perspective which is somewhat lacking in our studies on the Gita so far. And finally, we have also to answer the question as to why the commentators and poet-saints who wrote on the subject of the Gita, during the ancient and medieval periods of our history, stressed the importance of Jnana or Bhakti but there had been none worthy of mention who may be said to have exposed its way of Karma? Most of them were in favour of upholding and preserving the traditional values, not to talk of any new interpretation so as to bring any effective change in the prevailing conditions of the society.[34] The general attitude towards the Gita, as correctly put by D.D. Kosambi, is "honoured more often than read and understood less than it is recited".[35] We have also to explain why Karmayoga received due attention only during the modern period of our history? Is it because of the development of scientific attitude, which was, in fact, an impact of the introduction of the western system of education? Scientific temper has given great impetus to human activities all over the world. Had this temper awakened in India earlier, the entire course of our history would probably have been completely changed.[36]

Notes

1. B.G. Tilak, *Srimadbhagvadgitarahasya athava Karmayogashastra*, original Marathi Edition, Poona, 1915, Appendix, pp.505-88; S. Radhakrishnan, *The Bhagavadgita*, George Allen and Unwin (India), 1971, Introductory Essay.

2. *Collected Works of Sir R.G. Bhandarkar*, Poona, 1927-33, I, pp.209-13; K.T. Telang, *Selected Writings and Speeches* (ed.) V.N. Naik, Bombay, Vol.II, pp.1-175, "Bhagavadgita: Originality and Antiquity", Introductory Essay.
3. Radhakrishnan, *op.cit.*
4. Jnaneshvari (Bhavarthadipika); for details see V.L. Bhave, *Maharashtra Sarasvata*, Bombay, 1963, pp.104-22, Appendix. pp.715-26 (S.G. Tulpule).
5. Radhakrishnan, *op.cit.*, p.13, fn. 3.
   Sarvopanishado gavo dogdha Gopalanandanah
   Partho vatsah sudhir bhokta dugdham Gitamrtam mahat.
   (Vaishnaviya Tantrasara)
6. K. Antonova, G. Bongard-Levein, G. Kotovsky, *A History of India*, Moscow, 1979, I, p.149.
7. H.A. Phadke, "Srimadbhagavadgita: Central Philosophy and Relevance" in *Gita Jayanti Smarika*, Kurukshetra, 1999, pp.144-45.
8. Antonova, Levin and Kotovsky, *op.cit.*, p.150.
9. B.G. Tilak, *op.cit.*, Introduction.
10. H.A. Phadke, *op.cit.*, p.145.
11. *Ibid.*, pp.141-42.
12. V.N. Datta and H.A. Phadke, *History of Kurukshetra*, Kurukshetra, 1985, p.7; S.S. Chitrav, *Bharatavarshiya Charitrakosha*, Poona, 1964, I, pp. 230-32.
13. *Aparokshanubhuti* as quoted by Radhakrishnan, *op.cit.*, p.96, fn.1.
    Notpadyate vina jnanam vicarenanyasadhanaih
    Yatha padarthabhanam hi prakasena vina kvacit.
14. Radhakrishnan, *op.cit.*, p.96.
15. J. Krishnamurti, *Commentaries on Living*, London, 1976, "The Individual and Society", pp.30-32.
16. Radhakrishnan, *op.cit.*, p.12.
17. Aldous Huxley, in *Introduction to the Bhagavadgita*, by Swami Prabhavananda and Christopher Isherwood (1945).
18. Radhakrishnan, *op.cit.*
19. *Ibid.*, pp.13-14.
20. H.A. Phadke, *op.cit.*, pp.141-46.
21. *Ibid.*, p.146.
22. *Ibid.*, R.S. Sharma, *Material Culture and Social Formations in Ancient India*, Macmillan India Limited, 1985 (Reprint) Chs. I and II.
23. *History of Kurukshetra* "The Antiquity", pp.1-18.
24. *Ibid.*, pp.14-15.
25. *Ibid.*, p.4; Manu, II, 20.

26. *Ibid.*, p.23.
27. *Ibid.*, p.18.
28. H.A. Phadke, "Kurukshetra: Archaeology and Early History", Panjab University Research Bulletin (Arts), Vol.XXI, No.2, 2 October, 1990, p.173; *Haryana: Ancient and Medieval*, pp.29-31, Delhi, 1990.
29. *Gita Jayanti Smarika*, 1999, p.146, fn.41. As explained by Tarapad Choudhury (see his paper "The Vedas" in *History of Philosophy: Eastern and Western*, (ed.) S. Radhakrishnan et. al, London, 1957, Second Impression, p.45). "Rta invested the moral order with sublimity and inviolability and its working with inevitability and justice anticipating thus the 'doctrine of Karma'. Other terms used in the Vedas are Vrta which meant divine ordinance, including conduct, Satya agreement with reality and Anrta negation of Rta later restricted to truth and falsity of speech respectively, appear in moral context to represent virtue and vice generally."
30. *Ibid.*, pp.146-47.
31. *Ibid.*, p.147.
32. *Bharati* (Prof. R.C. Majumdar Volume), 1985-87, No.16, Banaras Hindu University, pp.257-63 for H.A. Phadke's paper "The Kurus in the Jatakas" and also *Haryana: Ancient and Medieval*, pp.29-31.
33. For a comparative study of the Gita and Buddhism see B.G. Tilak's *Gitarahasya*, pp.565-79, particularly the portion dealing with Arhat and Sthitaprajana, Nirvana and Moksha. Tilak draws our attention to an observation in Taranath's *History of Buddhism* (in Tibetan) and its English rendering as provided by Dr. Kern which is as follows: Nagarjuna was a pupil of the Brahmana Rahulbhadra, who himself was a Mahayanist. This Brahmana was much indebted to the sage Krishna and still more to Ganesh.

    "This quasi-historical notice", remarks Dr. Kern, "reduced to its less allegorical expression means that Mahayanism is much indebted to the Bhagavadgita and more even to Saivism". (*Manual of Indian Buddhism*, p.122; S.B.E., Vol.XVI, Intro. XXV-XXVIII).
34. *Gita Jayanti Smarika*, p.147.
35. D.D. Kosambi, *The Culture and Civilization of India in Historical Outline*, London, 1965, p.209.
36. *Gita Jayanti Smarika*, *op.cit.*

2

Krishna Dvaipayana Vyasa: The Founder of Indian Historical Tradition

In the Remembrance of History

Krishna Dvaipayana Vyasa is the editor of the Vedas, the author of the Mahabharata and the Bhagavata, the promulgator of all the Puranas and the expounder of the Vedanta. In fact, he thus laid the foundations of Indian historical and cultural traditions. This may perhaps be the reason why special homages are paid to him every year on the full moon day of Ashadha, very rightly designated as Vyasa Purnima or Guru Purnima. The Puranic declaration that he is the very incarnation of the all pervasive Lord Vishnu and the store-home of the supreme wisdom (Brahma-vidya)[1] and the popular belief that he survives till the dissolution of the universe[2] only suggest the universality of his greatness.

The Sources

Our main sources of information on the life and work of this great sage are the Mahabharata, the Bhagavata followed by their commentaries, the Vyasa legacy as gathered from the Puranas and their commentaries, the notices found in classical literature, the Brahmasutras and their great commentators,

Shankara, Ramanuja and Madhva. These sources provide Vyasa's brief biographical and personal details, his different names and their derivations, his personality-appearance and its sanctifying effect. He is the arch-type of a *muni* says the Gita[3] and in the epic itself and elsewhere he is verily Lord Narayana personified,[4] as none else could have composed that remarkable work. The greatness of Vyasa and his rich contributions as brought out in the classical literature in its typical poetic style draws our special attention.[5] In some of these remarks, Valmiki and Vyasa are mentioned together and compared with sun and the moon respectively.[6]

Vyasa's Names: Their Historical Import

The earliest reference to Vyasa occurs in the Taittiriya Aranyaka (1.9.2) in connection with his speculations on the concept of death (*mrtyu*).[7] According to Samaveda Brahmana, he was the disciple of Vishvaksena whose further genealogy is traced in that text.[8] We are mainly indebted to the Mahabharata and the Puranas for little more recollections on the life-story of this saintly personage. He was the son of Parasara and Satyavati and was born on an island in the vicinity of the river Yamuna and hence came to be known as Dvaipayana also called Parasharya.[9] As he had a very dark complexion he got the appellation Krishna found in Bhagavata along with his other names Satyavatisuta and Badarayana, the last because he was born in a forest where grew the *badari* (a fruit) trees.[10] The Vayu and the Vishnudharmottara Puranas designate him as Purana-Pravakta (an exposer of the Puranas)[11] while the Mahabharata associates his name Vyasa to his expansion and codification of the Vedic Samhitas.[12] The term Vyasa thus denotes a classifier, coordinator, compiler and an editor of the Vedas. The tradition has it that Lord Himself performs this work, in every Dvapara Age,[13] considering the limitations of humanity. It was Vyasa who gave to the Hindus their great religious texts in a classified and ordered form. He took up the floating mass of religious literature in the form of hymns and ritualistic instructions and classified them in four Vedas. Vyasa set up *asramas* and with the help of his four disciples, namely, Paila (Rigveda), Jaimini (Samaveda), Vaishampayana (Yajurveda) and Sumantu (Atharvaveda) who performed this stupendous editing work.[14] His son Shuka, later, became the heir to all this wisdom of the age. Vyasa thus represents the universal spirit beyond time and space and hence it would not be possible to fully measure the details of his life-work as presented in the sources mentioned above. Vyasa was also the progenitor of the line of the Bharatas immediately after Vichitravirya, a fact which shows that despite all his learning he was a human being and was attached to progeny. This adds a human perspective to his outstanding and superhuman personality.

The Brahmasutras

The basis of the various systems of the Vedanta philosophy we owe to the Brahmasutras of Badarayana.[15] Perhaps his idea in the composition of this work was to put the Upanishadic philosophy on a sound and precise footing for all time but he was also aware of the differing views which may occur while investigating on this subject.[16] This was a characteristic feature of Vyasa's all comprehending intellect (Vishala-Buddhi). The great commentators on the Brahmasutras-Shankara, Ramanuja and Madhva had paid glowing tributes to Vyasa in their respective works.[17] Ramanuja fulfilled the intense desire of his predecessor Yamunacharya to preserve the names of Parashara and Vyasa. In the Madhva tradition monasteries were built commemorating the glory of Vyasa. One such monastery is referred to by Vadiraja Yati, himself a follower of Shri Madhva, where the great Acharya had installed an icon of Vyasa. There are sculptures of Vyasa in Kanchi, in Varadaraja temple and the Vyasa Srantasraya.[18]

The Bharata Savitri

The Mahabharata, also called Bharata Savitri in the Kumbhakonam edition, is perhaps the most widely known contribution of Vyasa. He was an eye witness to the great battle which forms the central theme of his work. But for the Bharata, the world would have been blind. Truth and immortality constitute its body and to those who have listened to it, there is no more enjoyable thing that will appeal.[19] "Uphold Dharma, from it will flow whatever you need of Artha and Kama" proclaims the Bharata Savitri.[20] Every work is contained in it, as everything is in ether; and there is no story going about which does not derive sustenance from it, even as there is no body which can subsist without food. It is a treasure-house even as the ocean or the Himalayas. Indeed what is in it is found elsewhere and what is not in it cannot be found elsewhere.[21]

Parashara himself explained that none but the Lord himself could have composed this encyclopaedic work. It is called the bright lamp of wisdom, the brush that clears the vison of everyone. As the Bharata war was a great national calamity Vyasa, who survived it, should have deemed it necessary to preserve in this work "all traditional lore which might have already assumed a literary form".[22] It encompasses the culture and thought of the whole humanity. Its wealth of narratives, depth of spiritual insight, ethics and morality as gleaned from the Bhagavadgita, Vishnusahasranama, Viduraniti, Shanti and Anushasanaparvas, are relevant and sure guides even in modern times. As remarked by Sri Aurobindo:[23]

> Vyasa's supreme intellect rises everywhere out of the mass of insipid or turbulent redaction and interpolation with bare and grandiose outlines. A wide searching mind, historian, statesman, orator, a deep and keen looker into ethics and conduct, a subtle and high-aiming politician, theologian and philosopher, it is not for nothing that Hindu imagination makes the name of Vyasa loom so large in the history of Aryan thought and attributes to him a work so important and manifold. The wideness of the

> man's intellectual empire is evident throughout the work; we feel the presence of the great Rishi, the original thinker who has enlarged the boundaries of ethical and religious outlook.

Like Valmiki, Vyasa did not have occasions to show his poetic skill quite often for he was bound by the nature of his subject but was not altogether devoid of it either. Later poets have linked them both as incomparable poets of the land.[24] In the Adiparva, Lord Brahma praises Vyasa for his mystical knowledge and considers him superior to Vasistha, the great sage of yore, celebrated for his austerities.

> The darkness of men's minds have dispelled by the solar light of the Bharata which contains an exposition of Dharma, Artha, Kama and Moksha, both in concise and expanded form. The flaming lamp of Itihasa destroys the veil of Moha and illuminates the (heart-like) inner cell of the shrine of the world.[25]

The unity in diversity as gleaned through various forms of divine worship including the Pancharatra as related in the epic had a special role in reconciliation, assimilation, and integration of Indian culture; Vyasa was a universal friend for all ages. "His was not the light to be kept hidden in a bushel – it is to blazon over from the mountain top. But alas! the epic ends with a sad note that no one listens to the counsel of Dharma."[26] How true it is even to the times we are living in!

Bhagavatam Rasamalayam

Even after the compilation of the Vedas, and the composition of the Mahabharata, Vyasa's inner dissatisfaction did not wither away. While reflecting over the problem came the realisation that essential nature of the Self has not been really understood and that the ways of devotion (*bhakti*) to the Lord, dear even to the supreme renouncers, have not been dealt with fully. At the instance and advice of the sage Narada, Vyasa, sitting in a meditative mood in his asrama on the Sarasvati, composed the Bhagavatam, the scripture *par excellence*, of the devotion to

Lord Vishnu. Later he transmitted it to his worthy son Shuka, who recited it to King Parikshit for his ultimate liberation.[27] This work, universally acknowledged as the *magnum opus* of Bhagavata religion and philosophy, has inspired innumerable works in various languages of the world. Like the Gita, it has also brought out the harmonious blending of the three ways of self-realisation, i.e., Jnana, Bhakti and Karma, suited to the limitations of each aspirant. The central theme of the Bhagavatam is exposed at the very beginning in its rousing call:[28]

> Come all of you (of this world) who have taste and true feeling and drink the compact sweetness that is the Bhagavatam; the fruit of the Kalpataru, the Veda which has slipped down from the mouth of Shuka and is pure ambrosia.

The Purana Pravakta

Next to the Mahabharata come the Puranas, originally designed by Vyasa in his comprehensive style of narration, are considered indispensable for proper understanding of the Vedas, sometimes even extolled as of equal or even greater importance than the Vedas.[29] According to the *Skanda*, "the Purana contains things not contained in Sruti and Smrti", while the *Matsya* states that "the Puranas issued forth from the mind of Brahma first and then the four Vedas".[30] Especially for the Kali Age there is no greater Dharma than their propagation and reading and listening to their exposition.[31] The number of Vyasas according to the Puranas is twenty-eight, the last being Krishna Dvaipayana. This Vyasa genealogy is traced in the Puranas with several variations.[32] We are grateful to the Puranas for providing some biographical information on Krishna Dvaipayana. Narada and Sarasvati were instrumental in inspiring Vyasa in his tremendous task of the compilation of the Puranic lore.[33]

Scholars have placed the Puranas under the Agama class of literature. The Puranas do not differ basically from the aims and ideals of the Vedas and the Upanishads, i.e., the Nigamas. They are, in fact, complimentary to the exposition of the Vedas and hence have a place of honour in Indian religious consciousness.[34] Hinduism as a system of religions had no single founder or formulator. As a matter of fact, it is an outcome of the deep meditation of innumerable sages and philosophers through the ages. In the formulation of our religious consciousness Vyasa and Krishna, the inseparable combination, has indeed played a dominant role. The growth of our Agamic and Nigamic literature was due to the rich contributions of the scholars belonging to the tradition founded by Vyasa. Vyasa and a group of his disciples like Lomaharshana and Ugrasravasa Sauti, collected and disseminated sacred and historical traditions which were current among the people.[35] This mass of literature was related to cosmology (*sarga and pratisarga*), division of time (*manvantara*), genealogies of seers and sages (*vamsha*) and the legendary and historical accounts of various royal dynasties (*vamshanucharita*), all such matter may be called the basic or the original Purana.[36] In course of time, legends and traditions of the country generally came to be designated as Puranas. The Puranas which are eighteen in number, along with the Upapuranas, represent ancient Indian historical tradition. Vyasa must have at least compiled and edited the original Purana. In the estimation of Winternitz:[37]

> The Puranas are valuable to the historian and to the antiquarian as sources of political history by reason of their genealogies. At all events they are of inestimable value from the point of view of the history of religion, and on this head alone deserve far more careful study than hitherto been devoted to them. They afford us far greater insight into all aspects and phases of Hinduism... than many other works.

And in the words of Pargiter, the Puranas "may be described as a popular encyclopaedia of ancient and medieval Hinduism, religious, philosophical, historical, personal, social and political".[38] In his *Discovery of India,* Pt. Nehru wrote:

"Indian mythology is richer, vaster, very beautiful and full of meaning. I have often wondered what manner of men and women they were who gave shape to these bright dreams, and lovely fancies and out of what gold mines of thought and imagination they dug them."[39] The Puranic mythology and legends have made a deep impact on popular mind – they have in fact, become a part of Indian cultural life.

Homages to Vyasa

The continuity of the Indian historical and cultural traditions as well laid by Krishna Dvaipayana Vyasa is brilliantly reflected in the homages paid to his sacred memory by the Puranas, by the Acharyas of various schools of the Vedanta philosophy, by the commentators of the *Mahabharata*; and the Gita and by such outstanding classical writers as Kalidasa, Bana, Bharavi, Dandi, Kshemendra and others. V. Raghavan has done a commendable service to the researcher as well as the general readers, in publishing a collection of *Homages To Vyasa* (Sri Vyasa Prashastayah).[40] To conclude, we cannot but quote here from Kshemendra, himself a great devotee of Vyasa, as is suggested by the poets *aparanama* (alias) Vyasadasa in the colophon of his *Bharatamanjari.* The passage is remarkable for its vivid portrayal of Vyasa, his physical appearance, his unfathomable learning as also his immeasurable moral and spiritual level. It reads:[41]

> Vyasa's yellow matted hair resembles a mass of the flames of the fire of knowledge; he is dark in body but his splendour is free from darkness; the brilliance of his white beard has made the splendour of his body variegated; his eyes are like burning lamps capable of destroying the darkness (ignorance) of the three worlds; he is like a thousand-branched tree of the garden of dharma (virtues), bearing fruits of nirvana; he wears the skin of a black antelope, which looks like an array of black bees eager for the fragrance of his virtues; his white brahma-sutra or the sacrificial thread, resembles the digit of the moon; he is like the full

moon rising out of the ocean of Shastras filled by the rivers of Vidyas; he is like the essence of nector and is the creator of poetry. Salutation to Vyasa, the seat of truths; the abode of austerities, and the reliever of the fatigue of transmigration (or the mundane existence).

Notes

1. *Mahabharata* (Poona ed.), Adi. 4; (Kum. ed.) Adi. 1.32, Sa.356. 11,359, 4-6; Va. 1.43; Nar. 1, 17-18; Pad. 5.1, 43; Mat.185.30; Ku.1.51, 48-49.
   व्यासाय विष्णुरूपाय व्यासरूपाय विष्णवे।
   नमो वै ब्रह्मनिधये वासिष्ठाय नमोनमः॥
   Mahabharata
2. *Puranam,* Vol.VI, No.2, July, 1964 (Ramnagar, Varanasi), p.375, *Acharendunibandha* (Anandasrama ed.), Vyasavachanam.
   अश्वत्थामा बलिर्व्यासो हनुमांश्व विभीषणः।
   कृपः परशुरामश्व सप्तैते चिरजीविनः॥
3. *Bhagavadgita, 10.37,* मुनीनामप्यहं व्यासः।
4. See fn.1, above.
5. V. Raghavan, *Homages to Vyasa*, Ramnagar, Varanasi, 1963, pp.16-26.
6. *Ibid.*, pp.3,17; Danapala, *Tilakamanjari*, 20.
7. S.S. Chitrav, *Bharatavarshiya Prachina Charitrakosha,* Poona, 1932, p.557.
8. *Ibid.*
9. *Ibid.*, pp.557-58; *Mahabharata* (Kum. ed.), Adi. 60.2; 64.126.
10. *Bhag.* 4.40; 1.7.3; 9.22.35; Chitrav, *op.cit.*
11. Chitrav, *op.cit.*; *Va.* 1.1; 1.60; 11-21; 2.9.84; *Vis.Dh.*, 1.74.
12. *Mahabharata Ad. 64.130* (Kum. ed.); *Chitrav, op.cit.*
    विव्यास वेदान् यस्मात्स तस्माद्व्यास इतिस्मृतः।
13. *Vis.*, 3.3.5; *Na.* 1.17-18.
14. Chitrav *op.cit.*, pp.559-61; S.V. Ketkar (ed.), *Maharashtriya Jnanakosha,* II, *Vedavidya*, Bombay, 1921, "Veda ani Vyasa", p.12.
15. Chitrav, *op.cit.*, p.558; *Mahabharataki Namanukramanika*, Gita Press, Gorakhpur, Sam.2016, "Vyasa", pp.330-33.
16. Chitrav, *op.cit.*, p.561 for a brief statement of different views on the identification of Badarayana.
17. V. Raghavan, *op.cit.*, p.27, Chitrav, *Bharatavarshiya Madhyayugina Charitrakosha*, pp.599, 706; paying his tribute Shankaracharya wrote:
    अपान्तरतमा नाम वेदाचार्यः पुराणर्षिः विष्णु नियोगात्
    कलिव्दापरयोस्सन्धौः कृष्ण -

व्दैपायनस्संबभूव इति स्मरन्ति। तेषां अपान्तरतम:
प्रभृतीनां वेदप्रवर्तनादिषु लोकस्थितिहेतुषु अधिकारेषु
नियुक्तानाम् अधिकारतन्त्रत्वात स्थिते:।

ब्रम्हसूत्र शांकर, 3.3.32

18. *Valmiki and Vyasa*, Publication Division, New Delhi, 1992, p.54 (R. Rangachari's paper Veda-Vyasa).
19. V. Raghavan, op.cit., pp.37-47 "Glory of the Mahabharata".
20. *Ibid.*, p.3.
21. *Mahabharata* (Poona) *1.2.238, 240; 1.1.209; 1.56. 27,33.*
अस्याख्यानस्य विषये पुराणं वर्तते व्दिजा:।
अन्तरिक्षस्य विषये प्रजा इव चतुर्विधा:॥
अनाश्रित्यैतदाख्यानं कथा भुवि न विघते।
आहारमनपाश्रित्य शरीरस्यैव धारणम्॥
महत्वाद्भारवात्वाच्च महाभारतमुच्यते।
निरूक्तमस्य यो वेद सर्वपापै: प्रमुच्यते॥
यथा समुद्रो भगवान्यथा च हिमवान गिरि:।
ख्यातावुभौ रत्ननिधी तथा भारतमुच्यते॥
धर्मेचार्थे च कामेच मोक्षेच भरतर्षभ।
यदिहास्ति तदन्यत्र यन्नेहास्ति न तत्क्वचित्॥
22. R. Rangachari, *op.cit.*, p.46.
23. *Ibid.*, 4.47; Sri Aurobindo, *Vyasa and Valmiki*, "The Genius of Vyasa" in *Puranam*, Vol.III, No.2, 27 July, 1961, pp. 192-94.
24. V. Raghvan, *op.cit.*, pp.17,19,21 for reference to Danapala (*Tilakamanjari* 20), Kaviraja *(Raghavapandaviya,* 1,7,9,11,36,42) and Kalidasa (Sukti).
25. *Mahabharata* (Poona), Adi. Appendix. I, p.885, English rendering by Dr. V.S. Agrawala in *Purana*, Vol.I, No.2, Feb. 1960, pp.123-24.
इतिहास प्रदीपेन मोहावरणघातिना।
लोकगर्भगृहं कृत्स्नं यथावत् संप्रकाशितम्॥
26. *Mahabharata* (Kum. ed.), *Svargarohana, 5. 75-76.*
ऊर्ध्वबाहुविरौम्येष न च कश्र्वित्श्रृणोति मे।
धर्मादर्थश्र्व कामश्र्च स किमर्थ न सेव्यते॥
न जातु कामान्न भयान्नलोभात्
धर्मं त्यजेज्जीवितस्यापि हेतो:।
नित्योधर्म: सुखदु:खे त्वनित्ये
जीवो नित्यो हेतुरस्य त्वनित्य:॥
27. *Bhag.*, 1.7; *Pad.* Uttara, 198; Chitrav, *op.cit.* p.558; R.Rangachari, p.51.
28. *Bhag.* 1.13 *Kalyana*, Vol.16, No.2, Gorakhpur, September, 1941.
निगम कल्पतरोर्गलितं फलं शुकमुखादमृत द्रवसंयुतम्।
पिबत भागवतं रसमालयं मुहुरहो रसिका भुवि भावुका:॥
29. V. Raghavan, *op.cit.*, pp.3-4; Skand, Prabhasa, 2.90, 92; Reva, 1.18,19,20,23.
30. *Mat.* 53. 3,4; *Nara.* 2. 24.17; *Brahmanda*, 1.170, 171.

31. *Shiva.* Uma, 13.31, 35-41.
32. *Mat.*, 52. 3-11; 200. 31-32; *Ling.* 1.24; Chitrav, *op.cit.*, p.558, V.Raghavan, *op.cit.*, Appendix, genealogical list of names of the twenty-eight Vyasa.
33. Chitrav, *op.cit.*, pp. 558-61; *Mahabharata-Ki-Namanukramanika,* "Vyasa", pp.330-33; Devi. Bha. 1.3; *Mahabharata* Adi. 64-131 (Kum. ed.); *Bhag,* 12:4; *Skan.* 2.3.7, *Yayu 1.1, Brah.* 26; *Ganesha.* 1.12; *Bhavi. Brah. 1.60.*
34. *Puranam,* Vol.I, No. 1, July, 1959, pp.10-15 for Dr. Suniti Kumar Chatterji's article on "The Puranas".
35. *Ibid.*
36. For a detailed discussion on the characteristics of Purana with reference to various sources, see Pt. Giridhar Sharma Chaturvedi's paper "Purana – Lakshanani" in *Puranam,* Vol.I, No.2, February 1960, pp.130-38.
37. M. Winternitz, *A History of Indian Literature,* Vol.I, p.629; *Puranam,* July, 1959.
38. E.E. Pargiter, *Encyclopaedia of Religion and Ethics,* X, p.448; Purana, July, 1959.
39. *The Discovery of India*, Oxford University Press (India), 1992, p.78.
40. V. Raghavan, *op.cit,*
41. Kshemendra, *Bharatamanjari,* Kavyamala 64, pp.850-51, verses 13-20; *Puranam,* Vol.VI, No.2, July 1964, pp.261-63 (Anand Swarup Gupta).

3

The Problem of Dating Early Indian History

Chronology had been the weakest point of our early history as our forebears have left only a traditional literary account. We are grateful to the Greek historians for providing the starting point of our chronology. Although not conscious, they had done it while giving us an account of Alexander's Indian campaigns and also those Bactrian Greeks who followed him. Still we are not on any firm ground for dating Indian historical process before Alexander.

In view of this, one gets surprised to see an advertisement appearing in the *Times of India*, dated 10 December 1999, sponsored by the Education Department of the Ministry of Human Resources and Development, Government of India. The advertisement, it is supposed, is primarily meant to draw attention of academicians as well as the people, to the programme through the year for the propagation of the Sanskrit language and culture. Sanskrit had been, from the remote past, the chief medium of our cultural heritage and any administrative measure for its promotion should be most welcome. However, the intention seems to be publicising along with the Sanskrit year, the idea of Yugabda 5101 and the consequent rewriting of Indian history. According to us this is not acceptable for the reasons as follows:

First, we would like to know and legitimately so, whose brainchild is this and what is his standing in the field of historiography, specially when it has yet to receive attention of serious students of historiography in India and abroad. Second, the theory is built mainly on astronomical calculations and casual references in a few inscriptions of a much later period. It is based on three assumptions namely, the date of the Bharata Battle, the accession of Yudhisthira and its reckoning called Yudhisthira Samvat and the beginning of the Kali Age. All are interrelated and interdependent.

How controversial and difficult has been the problem of historicity and the date of the Bharata Battle can very well be understood from the volume *Mahabharata: Myth and Reality*. The controversy was started by D.C. Sircar in his address at the Bhandarkar Oriental Research Institute, Pune and which received full support from Sankalia of the Deccan College, Pune. It was challenged by us in a press-note and also in its following rejoinders.

In view of the above it would be necessary to settle the historiocity of the Mahabharata war first, and then take up the problem of fixing its approximate time bracket.

The Historicity of the Mahabharata Battle

Those who question the historicity of the Mahabharata war do so on the ground that there is no direct literary and archaeological evidence establishing its reality, and they go further by disregarding the veracity of the Puranic tradition, and highlighting the 'interpolative' character of the Mahabharata. In the reconstruction of the period of our ancient Indian history when our forebears did not demonstrate a strong historical sense, and did not record events like the Greeks, we ought to be circumspect in treating the evidence with an imaginative sympathy and judicious scrutiny. Two points must be made at the outset – first, as the war took place after the composition of *Rigveda*[1] there could, therefore, be no possibility of its being mentioned in the early Vedic literature. For one thing,

Vyasa, the compiler of the Vedas was also the author of the Mahabharata. So possibly he was resisting the temptation of duplicating his task. Secondly, the Vedic literature belonged to a different category of work in which religious matters tended to gain primary importance.[2]

The site of Kurukshetra as a battlefield is significant because it had enjoyed the reputation as a battlefield prior to the Mahabharata war, and this reputation continued even thereafter. Earlier it had been the scene of the tribal conflicts of the Aryans and the non-Aryans as reflected in the hymns describing the battles of King Sudasa.[3] It was here that Bhargava Parashurama fought Bhishma.[4] The martial qualities of the people of this region were also recognised later by the *Manusamhita* which recommends the placing in the van of battle, men born in Kurukshetra together with those of Matsya, Panchala and Surasena.[5]

The opening verse[6] of the Mahabharata refers to a historical poem called *Jaya* (victory) which was composed by Vyasa, a contemporary of the heroes of the war. This poem alludes to the strife between the rivals, Kauravas and Pandavas which Vyasa witnessed. This work is unfortunately lost (?), but it did exist once is clearly gathered from the epic. The early Vedic literature[7] refers to a number of rulers, like Shantanu, Vichitravirya and Dhrtarashtra later described in the Puranas as ancestors of the epic heroes, and Devakiputra Krishna[8] and Shikhandin Yajnasena[9] (the direct participants), suggesting thereby their involvement in the war. Sankhayana and Ashvalayana (*c.* 800-600 B.C.) the well-known *Sutrakaras*, the two early authorities were well-acquainted with the war. Sankhayana mentions a sacrificial error which had brought misfortune to the Kurus by driving them out of Kurukshetra.[10] Ashvalayana's knowledge of the event is evident from his reference to Vaishampayana, a pupil of Vyasa as *Bharatacharya*.[11] Panini[12] (*c.* 500 B.C.), the distinguished grammarian, mentions, curiously enough, in his disquisition on grammar, the names of Vasudeva, Arjuna, Bhima, Bhishma,

Yudhisthira, Kunti and Kurus who were connected with the Mahabharata war. He is acquainted with Vyasa and his pupils Paila and Vaishampayana. This extraordinary collection of names at one place though made for a different purpose denotes the particular type of relationship in which these personalities were involved, and which became a theme of the epic. Patanjali[13] (*c.* 200 B.C.), another noted grammarian, similarly refers to Bhima, Nakula and Sahadeva. Kautilya (*c.* 400 B.C.) attributes the destruction of Duryodhana to his usurpation of another's (Pandava's) kingdom.[14] This literary tradition extended over for more than a thousand years has persisted down the centuries particularly in a number of places in Kurukshetra studded with memories of the Bharata war.

The earliest Puranas[15] (5th-4th century B.C.) consider the war as a dividing line between two great epochs – *Dvapara* and *Kali*, i.e., past and present, and their genealogical portion which does not mention the next generation of the Kauravas (thereby suggesting their extinction) continues the Bharata Kuru genealogy only in the line of Arjuna, third of the Pandavas. This also finds corroboration in the Buddhist literature[16] which refers only to Dhananjaya and kings of the Yudhisthira stock. The Puranas affirm quite distinctly that the Mahabharata war inaugurated a political era, and a new period of degradation from the cultural point of view.[17] The ruin of the Yadavas because of the fratricidal strife, the attack of the Abhiras on the forces of Arjuna, the Naga invasion of Hastinapura and the subsequent death of Parikshit illustrate the general decadence of the times. The Chinese pilgrim Hiuen Tsiang who visited Kurukshetra in 634 A.D., while referring to a popular tradition regarding the battle, states that "a terrible fight had taken place in the region of Thanesar in remote times so that the entire area was covered with bones which were still visible to him".[18] In the Puranas there is a reference to Asthipura or 'the city of bones' which Cunningham[19] has identified as the site where the cremation of those slain in the battle took place.

The archaeological evidence[20] in support of the Bharata war is indirect as B.B. Lal has shown.

The P.G. Ware associated with the Mahabharata period presupposes knowledge of iron technology, and the possibility of its use in warfare in some form cannot be altogether ruled out. Even if it is assumed that iron came in regular use in warfare at a later period it need not prevent a war being waged and won without it. The description of the war in the Mahabharata is no doubt exaggerated but to deny the historicity of the event on this count is unjustified.

According to the Mahabharata[21] the battle was fought at Samantapanchaka (another name for Kurukshetra) and seems to have extended over the area covering Kaithal, Pehowa, Amin, and Thanesar. This is confirmed by the local tradition which associates a number of places such as Banaganga, Amin, Karnaka-qila, Basthali, with the heroes and events of the war.

The Problem of Dating the Battle

The importance of the Bharata war date for the chronological reconstruction of the early history of ancient India is unquestioned. It is, in fact, one of those few topics of ancient India over which so much diversity of scholarly opinion has existed. This may be accounted for the conflicting nature of the evidence at our disposal – literary, archaeological and astronomical. But it is still possible, as shown by the recent controversy, to reinforce the literary evidence with archaeological finds, and to arrive at a reasonable date for the Bharata war.

The Vamsha or the list of teachers given in the *Shatapatha Brahmana,*[1] *Brihadaranyaka Upanisad*[2] *and Kaushitaki* or *Sankhayana Arnayaka*[3] suggests that Gunakhya Sankhayana, the well-known *Sutrakara*, flourished seven or eight generations after Parikshit who was born after the war. Sankhayana was a contemporary of Ashvalayana,[4] another renowned *Sutrakara*. Whether this Ashvalayana was identical with his namesake mentioned in the *Majjima Nikaya*[5] as a contemporary of Buddha cannot be said with certainty but it goes beyond doubt that the war was fought before Sankhayana and Ashvalayana (*c.* 800-600 B.C.), the early authorities on the subject.

The early Vedic literature mentions quite a number of rulers of the Bharata-Puru-Kuru line who are known to the Mahabharata as ancestors and predecessors of Parikshit. These rulers are: Pururavas Aila,[6] Ayu,[7] Yayati Nahushya,[8] Puru,[9] Bharata Dauhshanti,[10] Ajamidha,[11] Riksha,[12] Samvarana,[13] Pratipa,[14] Balahika Pratipeya,[15] Shantanu[16] and Dhrtarashtra Vaichitravirya.[17] Of these Shantanu mentioned in the 10th *mandala* of the *Rigveda* and Dhrtarashtra Vichitravirya of the *Kathaka Samhita* are of crucial importance in respect of their near contemporaneity to the Bharata war. Shantanu and Dhrtarashtra were the same known to the epic and Puranic tradition as the great grandfather and father of the Kauravas. Furthermore, the Vedic literature also mentions Devakiputra Krishna[18] and Shikhandin Yajnasena[19] (the direct participants) and Vyasa Parasarya[20] known to the earliest Puranas as the compiler of the Vedas, and also a contemporary of the Mahabharata heroes.

On linguistic grounds the composition of the Rigvedic hymns has been suggested as between 1500-1000 B.C.[21] On this basis the date of Shantanu referred to above may reasonably be fixed sometime in the early 12th or 11th century B.C. Counting from this point and considering the rules of the intervening generations, i.e., of Vichitravirya, regency of Bhishma and the long reign of Dhrtarashtra, it may be possible to date the Mahabharata war at about 1200-1000 B.C. This also provides a margin of a few centuries for the foundation and growth of Vedic culture after its assimilation with the late Harappan culture (*c.* 1500 B.C.).

Attempts at fixing the date of the battle were made for the first time by astronomers in the Gupta period because of the growth of scientific literature on that subject. But the date in the 4th, 3rd, and 2nd millennium B.C. is not compatible with our knowledge of the proto-historic period, i.e., the discovery of late Harappan settlements (2000-1500 B.C.) at a number of places such as Daulatpur, Karnaka-qila, Dudhkheri, Panditonka-Tila and Jogna Khera – all situated in the Kurukshetra region. Fixing the date in the 15th, 14th and 13th century B.C. goes against the accepted scheme of an average reign per generation between the war and King Udayana of the Puranic genealogy. The recent attempt to bring down the date of the war to the second half of the 9th century B.C. does not hold good.[22] It cannot be reconciled with the date of the composition of the *Rigveda* on linguistic considerations.

The battle was fought after the composition of the *Rigveda* on linguistic consideration, and the reference to Shantanu, Devapi and Dhrtarashtra as mentioned above in the early Vedic texts. In view of this, the date may be fixed within the time bracket of ± 1200-1000. We will, however, not be surprised if the Painted Grey Ware (PGW) in the Sarasvati basin, at sites like Bhagavanpura where juxtaposition between Vedic and late Harappan culture is found, and which may be dated to the 14th or 13th century B.C. allowing a couple of centuries for the early stage. This will receive additional support from recent discoveries made by the archaeologists of Pakistan in providing sequence of culture from Neolithic to the early Indo-Sarasvati civilisation thus setting at rest the foreign origin theory of the Aryans and their consequent invasion of India (S.P. Gupta, *The Lost Sarasvati and the Indus Civilization*, Jodhpur, 1995, p.193; *The Indus- Sarasvati Civilization: Origin Problems and Issues*, 1996, Delhi). Gupta and Ramachandran have ably refuted the view placing the war in pre-Mauryan period (*Mahabharata: Myth and Reality*, p.24). They wrote:

> Archaeologically speaking after the Harappans the first Indian cities were established not before the Mauryan period, since in terms of monumental structures, use of baked bricks, planned settlements, and above all, the writing, are conspicuous by their absence in the pre-Mauryan and post-Harappan levels. Then

should we take, the date of the original Mahabharata, which is also the actual date of the war, as Mauryan or post-Maurayan. No one would do that for several well-known reasons (see the note of Phadke in the monograph).

We have seen how on the basis of century-old literary tradition it is possible to trace the historicity of the battle, yet on its date it is not so in the absence of any positive evidence. After considering archaeological, epigraphic, literary and astronomical evidence it was observed that no decision could he taken on the issue for the evidence is not conclusive. Gupta and Ramachandran, while editing differing views on the subject, have also come around the view that in the present state of our knowledge no conclusion is possible, and any suggestion in favour of absolute dating of the event, would be simply an exercise in futility. Whether this miracle is possible by astronomical calculations or by the aid of its sister discipline astrology, remains outside the realm of scientific investigation.

It may be of interest to point out that among the scholars belonging to the discipline of mathematics and astrology, mention may be made of S.B. Roy who is well-known for his writings on Indian chronology based primarily on astronomical evidences. His study (*Date of the Mahabharata Battle*, The Academic Press, Gurgaon, 1976) coming as it is after the heated controversy of 1975-76 on the historicity and date of the Bharata war, is the author's latest contribution to the subject (see our review of the book in the *Sunday Standard*, of the *Times of India*, 16 October 1977).

Back to the Good Old War

The S.B. Roy's study is not, as one is likely to suppose, merely an inquiry into the problem of the date of the Mahabharata battle but to be more precise, a study of early Indian chronology and its allied problems.

The author has attacked Max Mueller's chronology based on wrong identification of Vedic Kabandhi Katyayana with

Vararuchi Katyayana. He is equally critical of Pargiter, Raychaudhuri and B.B. Lal for their dates of the Bharata war in 9th-10th century B.C. He has rightly pointed out that Raychaudhuri's identification of Siradhvaja Janaka, the father of Sita, with the Janaka of the Upanishads, and of Assalayana of the Buddhist literature with Ashvalayana, the famous Sutrakara, does not rest on solid foundation. The author has very ably demonstrated the comparative reliability of the Vamshanucharita sections of the Puranas, the Mahabharata (from Shantanu to Sarpasatra) and the Bhavishya Purana (of kings after Adhisimakrishna). As archaeology is of little help (so far) in dating the battle, the learned scholar emphasises the need of astronomical method which, according to him, is in corroboration with the Puranic tradition regarding Nanda's coronation (sometime in the middle of the 4th century B.C.) 1015 years (here the reading 1500 is excluded) after the date of birth of King Parikshit (1424 B.C.).

On the basis of astronomical references in literature, a chronological framework is provided wherein Baudhayana and the Sutra literature are placed in the 14th century B.C. It is argued that the date 1425-1414 B.C. for the battle would not be unreasonable for it must have preceded the Sutra period. Further, the king and rishi lists of the Puranas and the Brahmanas have been so adjusted so as to bring them in conformity with these conclusions.

The author's identification of Gautamiputra, a rishi mentioned in the Upanishads, with Gautam Buddha makes an amusing reading. The evidence of the Buddhist literature, our principal source of information on the biographical details of Buddha, does not seem to have been taken into account. Moreover, attention may be drawn here to the statements of the Vedic literature considering the Easterners (which obviously included the Shakyas also) as beyond the pale of Vedic civilisation. The learned scholar believes that the composition of the Vedic hymns ended in 1400 B.C. but this does not agree with his dating of the Sutra literature and the Bharata battle. In the first place, there is no gap left for the composition of the Brahmanas and the Upanishads; and secondly, we shall have to place the battle before the composition of the Vedic hymns, in which case its non-mention therein becomes inexplicable. The Krishna Devakiputra of the Chandogya may be identical with the Krishna of the Mahabharata but Devakiputra's further identification with Krishna Angirasa and Narayana of the Rigveda, as suggested by the author, does not seem to rest on evidence. Similarity of certain philosophical ideas need not be taken as evidence for drawing such an inference. If Krishna of Rigveda is identical with that of the Mahabharata, it may be asked as to why the Pandavas do not figure in the text. As suggested by us elsewhere (*Mahabharata: Myth and Reality*, pp. 188-94) the battle was fought after the composition of the Rigvedic hymns.

In two chapters which seem to be the core of the book, the author minutely examines the astronomical evidence in the Mahabharata which according to him belongs to the original layer. Using various methods, indirect astronomical as well as epigraphic evidence, the epoch of the battle is calculated as 1424-1414 B.C. While arriving at this date the author has done well in providing the outer (1716-1088 B.C.) and the inner (1482-1280 B.C.) margins. For the chronological reconstruction of our ancient past we depend on various sources and astronomy is of course, one of them. The astronomical evidence therefore, need not be considered in isolation but in correlation with more valid evidence of archaeology or contemporary literary tradition. And until the full report of the Bhagwanpura excavation is published and more archaeological sites associated with the epic story are excavated, no conclusion on the date of the Bharata battle could be reached with certainty.

But the most constructive part of the book is the author's search of the original Mahabharata based on a thorough analysis of its critical edition. The book is supplemented with two very useful appendices. The Aryan invasion(?) is suggested at about 2000-1900 B.C. after a careful consideration of the literary, archaeological, astronomical and cross-contact evidence. The 'Kurukshetra' appendix throws welcome light on some aspects of the history of the region. But the foundation of Kurukshetra attributed to King Kuru entirely on the basis of the Puranic evidence needs to be discarded in view of the statement of the Shatapatha Brahmana associating Pururavas, a remote ancestor of Kuru, with Kurukshetra. Further, the identification of Kurusravana, a Vedic king with Kuru Samvarana cannot be accepted both on linguistic and genealogical grounds. The evidence of the Rigveda referring to Mitratithi and Upamasravas as the father and son respectively of Kurusravana makes such identification absolutely unnecessary.

Despite this criticism the book may undoubtedly be regarded as a valuable contribution to the study of early Indian chronology.

* * *

The dating of the Mahabharata battle had always been a handy issue for the researchers of the traditional view which includes those in favour of Bharatiya Janata Party's view on history and their condemnation of all western historians without any discrimination. Their writings on Indian history and their unhistorical traditional interpretation was accepted because it admirably suits their ideology. Itihasa Samkalana Samiti was specially formed to rewrite Indian history from this angle. A critical survey of their publications on the Aryan problem and on western misconceptions about Indian history (They have no praise even for the writings of such liberal historians on Indian history and culture like Elphinstone, Havell, A.L. Basham and so many others) and their systematic attempts at establishing the great antiquity of our civilisation on the basis of their typical interpretation of the available sources, stressing exclusively the importance of the astronomical references because it suits their angle of interpreting Indian historical and cultural growth. In this process, the Yugabda 5101 theory of dating Indian history was born and was accepted at the highest level.

They have the audacity of even ignoring what Sir Bhandarkar has said in this context. The Professor wrote: "The nationalistic bias is more fatal to the historian's vocation, for it invariably leads to form prejudiced and unjustified conclusions."

The Yugabda 5101 Theory of Dating Indian History Challenged

Is it possible to reach any conclusion on such vital subject as the dating of events mainly on a particular type of evidence ignoring other valid evidences like archaeology and also the Puranic genealogies of the ruling dynasties, studied so meticulously by several scholars of national and international repute. We may mention here the commendable attempt of R.C. Raychaudhuri in tracing the Indian chronology from the accession of Parikshit (*Political History of Ancient India*, pp.35-36) which took place after the Bharata war. It is worthwhile to trace our chronology further back to the Battle of Ten Kings, mentioned in the Rigveda, on the basis of the same comparative and critical method of writing early Indian history. If some result is obtained by this method then it may be possible to say that the starting point of Indian chronology may be pushed a few centuries earlier than the Bharata battle.

It may be asked if the Yugabda theory was envisaged in our remote past then how is it that it was never put into practice? And why the Puranas although providing regnal periods of kings and dynasties, do not mention them in respect of the era in which they are supposed to have been placed? And what about the archaeological evidence which is our direct and main source of information on pre-historic, proto-historic and historical periods of our history? Further, we should also take into account such evidence specially from the area (i.e., Kurukshetra) where the battle was fought according to Indian literary tradition. It must be remembered that the main function of a tradition is to confirm, corroborate and strengthen the archaeological evidence. The archaeological evidence, therefore, cannot be conveniently ignored in favour of tradition, astronomical or literary material. It can also be argued that if the accession of Yudhisthira is to be taken as a landmark for dating Indian history then why not consider the case of Rama, Krishna and Buddha who have left dominating influence over the course of Indian culture and thought, throughout the ages. This besides, these personages also figure in Indian Traditional Chronological Order.

True, it is that even after fifty-two years of our independence, Christian calender, a remnant of the colonial rule, is still being generally used. We can understand the feelings behind the urge for its replacement by exclusively our own calender, but this would be achieved only by adopting a purely rational approach. Various differing views need to be considered and thoroughly probed before drawing any conclusion. Presently, we would only suggest a national debate on this vital subject of our history. We really do not know if members of our parliament are aware of the development mentioned above. Nevertheless, one thing should be made clear that Indian history cannot be written on preconceived notions in respect of its chronological framework which has to be prepared exclusively on universally accepted norms of historiography.

Notes

The Historicity of the Mahabharata Battle

1. See under sub-head 'The Problem of Dating the Battle'.
2. These comments are warranted because Dr. D.C. Sircar regards the absence of mention of the war in early Vedic literature as a decisive reason for doubting its reality.
3. *Rigveda*, VII, 18, 18-19.
4. *Mahabharata, Udyoga*, 5. 180-186.
5. *Manu*, VII, 193.

6. *Mahabharata*, Adi, 62.20; *Udyoga* 136. 18.
7. *Rigveda*, X.98, *Kathka Samhita*, X. 6.
8. *Chandogya Upanisad*, III. 17. 6; Weber, *Indian Literature*, 169.
9. *Kaushitaki Brahmana*, VII.4.
10. *Sankhayana Srauta Sutra*, III. 4 16. 10-13.
11. *Ashvalayana Grihya Sutra*, III.4.
12. II. 4.59; III. 3.130; 4.74; IV. I. 114, 169, 176; 3.104; VIII.395.
13. IV. I.4.
14. *Arthashastra*, I. 6.
15. *Matsya*, 273. 49-50; *Vayu*, 99, 428-29.
16. *Jatakas*, II. 366; III. 400; IV. 361, 450; VI.260, etc.
17. F.E. Pargiter, *Ancient Indian Historical Tradition*, 1962, pp.284-85.
18. *Buddhist Records of the Western World*, Trans. Samuel Beal, 1969.
19. *Archaeological Survey of India, Report*, XIV, 1970, p.94.
20. B.B. Lal, "Archaeology and the two Indian Epics", *Annals of the Bhandarkar, Oriental Research Institute*, LIV, 1973, Pts. I-IV, pp.1-8; *Ancient India, Bulletin of the Archaeological Survey of India*, 1955.
21. *Mahabharata*, Adi, 1.2.9.

The Problem of Dating the Battle

1. *S.B.* X.
2. *B.U.* VI.
3. *Adhyaya*, 15.
4. Sankhayana's teacher Kahola is honoured by Ashvalayana.
5. II 147.
6. *Rigveda*, X. 95; *Shatapatha*, XI. 5, 1.1.
7. *Rigveda*, 1.53.10; 11.14,7. etc.
8. *Ibid.*, 1.31.17; X.63.1.
9. *Ibid.*, VII 8.4; 18.13.
10. *Shatapatha*, XIII 5,4. 11-12; *Aitareya*, VIII.23.
11. *Rigveda*, IV, 44.6.
12. *Ibid.*, VIII. 68.15.
13. *Ibid.*, 51, 1.
14. *Athrvaveda*, XX. 129.2.
15. *Shatapatha*, XII. 9.3.3.
16. *Rigveda*, X. 98.
17. *Kathaka Samhita*, X. 6.
18. *Chandogya Upanisad*, III. 17.6; Weber, *Indian Literature*, P.169.
19. *Kaushitaki, Brahmana*, VII.4.

20. Macdonell and Keith, *Vedic Index* I, p.519; *Vayu,* 60, 12-16; *Vishnu,* III. 4, 7-10; *Brahmanda,* II, 34, 12-16.
21. A.L. Basham, *The Wonder that was India,* p.32.
22. B.B. Lal, "Archaeology and the Two Indian Epics", *Annals of the Bhandarkar Oriental Research Institute,* LIV, 1973, Pts. I-IV, pp.1-8; *Ancient India,* 10 and 11 (1954-55).

Select Bibliography

Agrawala, G.C. (ed.), *Age of Bharata War*, Banarasi Das, Delhi, 1979.

"Back to the Good Old War" (our review of the book in the Sunday Standard of *The Times of India*, 16 October, 1977).

Datta, V.N. and H.A. Phadke, *History of Kurukshetra*, Kurukshetra, 1985.

Gupta, S.P. and K.S. Ramachandran (ed.), *Mahabharata: Myth and Reality (Differing Views)*, Agam Prakashan, Delhi 1976.

Roy, S.B., *Date of Mahabharata Battle*, The Academic Press, Gurgaon (Haryana) 1976 (our review of the book, *The Sunday Standard*, October 16, 1977).

Sensarma, Major P., *Kurukshetra War: A Military Study*, 1975, Dhiren Roy, Darabari Udyog, Jessor Road, Gangapur.

Sircar, D.C. (ed.), *The Bharata War and Puranic Genealogies*, University of Calcutta, 1969.

"The Yugabda 5101 Theory of Dating Indian History Challenged", *Deshdoot Times*, 2 January, 2000; *Maharashtra Times*, 22 December, 1999; *Sakal*, 24 December, 1999.

4

Sati: A Historiographical Survey of the Practice of Widow-Immolation in Ancient India

Sati or the immolation of Hindu widows forms one of the major themes in the studies on the position of Indian women in modern times. The debate on the sati was initiated by western orientalists[1] and British officers[2] of the Utilitarian and Romantic schools in their anxiety to highlight the benevolent character of their administrative system for the justification of a foreign rule over India. Nevertheless the problem has been studied by Indian scholars against the background of the necessity of social reform. To Lord William Bentinck is assigned most of the credit for the abolition of this inhuman practice through legislative measures.[3] Could he achieve any worthy success it may be asked, had there been any slightest sanction to this practice in the Vedas, the highest authority for a Hindu on civil and legal matters? Would he not then have probably withdrawn his proposed measures as was done by his forerunner, Mountastuart Elphinstone, the Governor of the Bombay Presidency who is known to have himself prepared a Minute on the abolition of the sati?[4] Is it without any significance that Clause I of the Sati Regulations XVIII of the Bengal Code 4 (December, 1829) makes specific mention that the practice is "nowhere enjoined by the religion of the Hindus as an imperative duty" and that "on the contrary a life of purity and retirement on the part of the widow is more especially and preferably inculcated".[5]

For more than one hundred and fifty years the problem has been discussed by well-known Indologists, historians and social reformers. However, a cursory glance at the writings on this theme of our social history would suggest that although these have largely increased in numbers there is so far no work dealing exclusively with the genesis and growth of the custom of the sati through the ages particularly during the early periods of our history when the Dharmasutra texts were composed, which to this day form the basis of our religious beliefs and social practices.[6] There are, however, a few works more concerned with the British policy on sati and the attitudes of the reformers and the orthodox sections of the society rather than providing an analysis of various sources to find answer to the question why and how the Indian women were led to immolate themselves on the funeral pyre of their dead husbands. In view of this P.V. Kane's essay on the 'sati' forming a part of his monumental *History of Dharmashastra*, still holds ground and is indispensable for any researcher working on this problem.[7]

Sati has defied all periodisation. It has neither remained exclusively an academic issue. Despite the administrative measures and the untiring zeal of the social reformers it has not been finally abolished. In the controversy that followed the Deorala incident, history was evoked in justification or condemnation of this accursed social evil. Popular sentiments were touched and intellectual minds stirred. If the past has any relevance to the present, if history has any pragmatic value (which certainly does not lie in legitimatising an inhuman practice nor in seeking religious sanction for its rejection) then the emancipation of women should form the subject of our deepest concern, so very imperative to the progressive realisation of the growth of any society.

Any inquiry into the genesis and growth of the problem of sati, therefore, shall have to take into account the historiographical background. Various sources of information on the practice of sati related to different religious and social groups pertaining to various regions and periods of time, their bearing on the basic features of the Indian social structure namely, the family, property and marriage, the idealistic view of life, the impact of tradition on popular mind and its reaction to any constructive approach to social change – all need to be properly analysed and examined.

The debate on the sati began with interpretations of a few Vedic passages in favour or otherwise of the sanction of the custom in contemporary times. The orthodox section favouring sanction theory wanted to convey to the government that any interference in religious matters would have its repurcussions[8] while others, conversant with the scientific method of textual criticism and also convinced of the necessity of social reform, were desirous of strengthening the hands of the government in its measures for the abolition of the sati.[9] The passages in question run as follows:[10]

> O woman: raise yourself towards the world
> of living; you lie down near this departed
> (husband); come, this your wifehood of the
> husband who (formerly) held your hand and
> who loved you has (now) been fulfilled.

That the widow is asked to rise up becomes evident from the *Ashvalayana Grihyasutra* (IV.2.16-18) which specifies this duty to her brother-in-law or someone who can be the representative of her husband or a pupil or even an old servant. The meaning is explicitly conveyed in *Atharva-Veda* followed by *Tai-Ar*. The verse states:[11]

> O (dead) man: this woman choosing the world of the
> husband lies down by thee,
> the deceased, observing *the old universal*

> *custom*; bestow on her in this
> world offspring and wealth.

The passages referred to above show that the women of household of the departed used to go to the cremation ground, a practice which continued to the time when *Brhad-devata*, the *Ashvalayana Grhyasutra* and the *Baudhayana Pitramedha Sutras* where composed.[12] The passages formed part of the funeral rites wherein position of wife near the dead body is described, a procedure which is more specifically related in later Brahmanical texts. No slightest indication is there in this funeral procedure of the widow's burning herself on the pyre. The *Rigvidhana* (III.8.4) makes the meaning more clear while directing the brother-in-law to call back the wife of his sonless deceased brother when she is to ascend the pyre, for procreating a son of her, chanting the aforementioned Rigvedic passages.[13] Probably, the text had the practice of *niyoga* in mind. The Rigvedic passage symbolically describes, as rightly pointed out by Kane "what even in the days of the Rigveda was probably a tradition, viz., that in hoary antiquity a wife burnt herself with her husband" and that "in the time of Rigveda this practice had altogether ceased."[14] In the passage the practice of *niyoga* is implied when the departed is called upon to bestow on the wife, offspring and wealth. But these texts do not refer to the practice of sati at all. It may not be unreasonable to suggest that the widows in the days of the Rigveda had either to marry their brother-in-law or go in for *niyoga* in case the husband died without leaving a son. The *Grhyasutras* and the *Brhad-devata* do not approve of the burning of the widow.[15] These authorities have not explicitly mentioned the practice of *niyoga* but they do not seem to be unaware of it either. *Rigvidhana*, a comparatively late work takes it in that sense.[16] It would thus appear that the practice of sati had no sanction in the early Vedic literature. There is perhaps nothing we can add to what Kane has already observed. He wrote:[17]

> There is no Vedic passage which can be cited as incontrovertibly referring to widow burning then current nor is there any *mantra* which could be said to have repeated in very ancient times at such burning nor do the *grhyasutras* contain any direction prescribing the procedure of widow burning.

That the Vedas do not sanction sati but were aware of its existence in pre-Vedic times is a valuable piece of information for forming some idea about its early phases. The remnants of the earlier practice as discerned from the Vedic funeral procedure and recitations need a careful consideration. As has been shown by various scholars sati was not exclusive to Brahmanical religion, it owes its origin to the oldest religious ideas and superstitious practices of mankind in general. It was known to the Egyptians, the Chinese, the Greeks, the Germans, the Slavs, the Scythians and many other races and tribes of the ancient world.[18] Possibly it was also prevalent among the indigenous people with whom the Aryans came in contact in course of their expansion. The former culture was deep-rooted to be ousted easily and hence reconciliation was the only course open to the new people. Through inter-marriages both the cultures were assimilated. That the Aryans badly needed wives for replenishing the stock becomes evident by their frequent references to the women slaves captured from the subjugated people in the Vedic literatures. In view of this, the Aryans although not in favour of the burning of the widow allowed the practice to exist in a symbolic form merely as a remnant of a tradition of the bygone age. The origin of the practice of sati is lost in the mist of antiquity. It cannot be traced beyond the hypothesis we have made, until some positive clue is provided by archaeology.[19] It is not possible to accept Wilson's contention that it originated later than the Vedic period.[20]

The position of the widow in the Vedic family which did not require her to immolate herself needs to be explained next. The answer to the question lies in the widespread practice of *niyoga*. The Rigveda, as already shown, alludes to this custom which has been explained by Yaska, Manu, Vishvarupa and Medhatithi in that sense only.[21] Gautama, Vishvarupa and Baudhayana Dharmasutras, Kautilya and Naradasmriti approve of it under restrictions,[22] while Apastamba, Brhaspati and Manu condemn it,[23] the last in strongest possible term. *Mitakshara* and Apararka commenting on Yajnavalkya forbid the practice in the Kali age.[24] Brahmapurana is cited as a supporting authority.[25] It appears that during the age of the Dharmasutras, the practice of *niyoga* although put under restrictions continued but gradually started losing its utility till the time of Mitakshara and Apararka when it came to be totally prohibited. *Niyoga* was also a relic of the past originated probably due to the necessity of sons in the context of a tribal society wherein war was the main profession and was abandoned gradually in the succeeding period when the situation changed. The Mahabharata is replete with cases of *niyoga* but very sparing in its references to widow burning.[26] It seems that the practice of sati was originally confined to the Kshatriya class and hence its instances were rare. The evidence of the Mahabharata cannot be cited in favour of the existence of the sati. The examples of the wives of Vasudeva and Krishna and Madri cannot be reconciled with their chronological position some time towards the close of the Rigvedic or early later-Vedic period wherein sati was not a prevalent custom and the succeeding age of the Dharmasutras which does not provide evidence of the existence of that practice. On the other hand, the practice of *niyoga* which is profusely mentioned in Vedic literature and the Mahabharata and is also approved by the Dharmasutras though with restrictions, suggest the references to the sati as later additions to the epic text. Widow's right to inheritance was not generally recognised in ancient India (Yaska, Ap., Manu and Narada).[27] Yajnavalkya, Vishnu-dharmasutra and Katyayana are the earliest authorities which recognise this right.[28] In the early medieval times widow's right to property was better recognised than in the times of the early Sutra writers.[29]

The Brahmanical idea of indispensability of male progeny for the salvation of the departed souls did not find conformity with the Buddhist view of life which makes no distinction between male and female. The paucity of references to widows in the Buddhist literature leads to the inference that the widowhood was not attended with hardships.[30] The widows had the right to inherit property, a feature which surprisingly does not find mention in the Dharmasutras. The life was not a burden to them therefore, they were not anxious to end it prematurely by a recourse to self immolation. The widows preferred asceticism to gross secularism. Evidence regarding widow-remarriage or *niyoga* are scanty which discountenances its general prevalence in the Buddhist society.[31] In the Buddhist texts women are given a distinctive superior place as far as their religious status is concerned – they had their own *samgha* although not without restrictions for Buddha initially did not favour admitting Bhikhunis (nuns) to the Buddhist Church.[32]

In Jainism the status of women as compared to that in Buddhism was more respectable. They were placed on equal footing with men as far as the pursuit and achievement of religious ideals were concerned. The *Kalpa Sutta* speaks of the number of *Sadhavis* reaching prodigious proportions in the life time of Mahavira.[33] Although in the Digambara order they were not considered for attainment of *nirvana*; were even abused being called untrustworthy, troublesome, demon-like,[34] yet their status in general was far from being degraded. Their monastic life was covered under uniform rules along with men; they were granted religious freedom, enjoyed legal rights of inheritance and possession of property over the son. Not only a childless widow but even one with sons had absolute right over the property of the deceased husband. The Jaina law questions the mundane and spiritual indispensability of a son and allows a widow full freedom in matters of sanctioning grants to religious endowments.[35]

The early Buddhist and Jaina texts which incidently fall within the same chronological limits as that of the early Dharmasutras do not make any reference to the practice of the sati. Whether it came into vogue as suggested by Romila Thapar "in reaction to the socio-religious movements which did not approve caste distinctions and supported continuing participation of women in social roles as wives and widows, the measures which were not looked with favour by upper classes"[36] cannot be precisely answered. It may be pointed out that this suggestion was also made by Kane in the context of child marriage.[37] True it is, that the position of women was much respectable under Buddhism and Jainism but we must not forget that in both these religious systems a powerful section which included some of their masters, did not favour admittance of women to their respective monastic orders. In early stage of Buddhism the status of women did improve but later domination of men and subordination of women in family reasserted. Women are mentioned along with "animate and inanimate property of Brahmins" and the best among the wives is described as one "who is best ministered."[38] Unless some evidence about the number of women in the Buddhist and Jaina monasteries is gathered and percentage of those of the Brahmanical order joining them is ascertained no inference can possibly be drawn. Further, it has to be shown that the number of widows belonging to Brahmanical religion reached to a alarming proportion so as to necessitate sanction for the immolation of the widows on the funeral pyre of their husbands. Actually the practice of the sati had already come into vogue and its regular sanction came later. Similarly, Thapar's observation on the practice of *sallekhana* (or slow starvation)[39] prevalent among the Jainas would be of no help in explaining the non-mention of the practice of sati in Jaina texts. *Sallekhana* as defined by Samantabhadra is "a vow to be adopted for seeking liberation of the soul from the body as a religious duty during a calamity, severe famine, old age or illness from which there is no escape or against which there is no remedy"[40] and as explained by Umaswami should be "adopted most willingly and voluntarily without passion or mental weakness"[41] and hence it should be clearly distinguished from suicide which is weighed down by mundane considerations. May it be pointed out that the Brahmanical idea of the widow joining her husband in the heaven was also adopted by Jains later. About twenty-eight memorial stone inscriptions of sati from Bikaner dateable between Sam.1557 and 1866 convey this sense.[42] It is surprising that the Chinese Buddhist pilgrims who make keen observations on the customs and practices of various religious groups of India do not make any comment on the practice of sati which had come into vogue during the time of their visit. Buddhist and Jaina religious thought, although not without progressive trends, namely, disapproval of caste distinction and inequality of sexes, was basically concerned with metaphysical question of the ultimate liberation of the soul from bondage. Even the radical thinkers like Ajivikas and the Lokayatas although they vehemently attacked Brahmanical concepts of Karma, rituals and Varna system, did not provide any positive answer to the social problems of the day. Unfortunately, so little is known about the social views of these philosophers that we cannot say with any amount of certainty that "whether they remained true to the principle of rationalist radicalism not only in thought but also with regard to social questions".[43] They have not made any reference either to the position of women in society or to their degraded status.

The *Manusmriti* (*c.* 200 B.C. – 200 A.D.) is silent on the question of sati. It requires the widow to live a chaste life and if she has no son then alone is she permitted to obtain one through *niyoga* (IX.59-61). However, Manu condemns the latter practice (IX.64-68) for causing *varna-samakara* and therefore, in conflict with the ancient *dharma*. Brhaspati (*c.* 300-500 A.D.) makes a vain bid to explain the contradiction in Manu as lack of the *tapas* and knowledge of the former ages in men and women of the Dvapara and Kali ages, the two essential ingredients for the strict observance of the rules of *niyoga*.[44] Whatever may be the reasons for condemning the *niyoga*, the evidence surely testifies to its existence in former times. The Vishnudharmasutra (*c.* 100-300 A.D.) allows an option to the widow – she can either observe celibacy or should ascend the funeral pyre after the husband.[45]

In the historical period the earliest reference to the immolation of women is found in a Greek text (account of Strabo) of the first century B.C. basing its observation on earlier accounts (of Aristoboulos) of the fourth century B.C. It states: widows are burnt on the funeral pyres of their dead husbands among the Katheae (*Katha*).[46] Diodorus gives another account of sati, that of the wife of General Keteus who died fighting against Antigonos.[47] The early epigraphic evidence however, comes from Eran in Central India referring to the wife of Goparaja who immolated herself when her husband died in battle (A.D. 510).[48] It may be interesting to note that between these two instances, covering a time gap of more than eight hundred years, no other reference is available in favour of a clear sanction to the burning of the widows. The *Vishnudharmasutra* makes it optional and not binding.

The period between 500 A.D. and 1200 A.D. is very crucial in the history of the sati. Not only does it find mention in the commentaries on the Smritis but also frequently referred to in secular literature as well as in the epigraphic records. During this very period, instances are not lacking of widows of royal families donating property to religious beneficiaries. This may possibly indicate the doners' religious leanings or the general spirit of religious tolerance of the contemporary times but it would be very difficult to correlate it with the circumstances leading to the occurrence of the practice of sati.

In the literature of this period the act of sati is variously called as *sahamarana* (dying together) or *sahagamana* (going together) or *anvarohana* (ascending the funeral pyre) and also *anumarana* (where husband is cremated elsewhere). It is mentioned in the *Gathasaptashati* (VII.33), the *Brhatsamhita* (Ch.74 ed. by Kern), the *Kamasutra* (VI.3.53), in the *Harshacharita* (Ch.5) and the *Kadambari* (ed. Kane, Purvabhaga, para 177) of Bana, the *Rajatarangini,* (VI.107, 195; VII.103, 478, 481) of Kalhana, in the commentaries of Medhatithi and Vijnaneshvara, and also in the accounts of the Arab writers Sulaiman and Al-Beruni.[49] This besides, several inscriptions from Central India, Rajasthan, Nepal, Maharashtra and Karnataka suggest that the practice was well known during this period,[50] an observation which is also supported by the discovery of several sati memorial stones. In a recent study (S. Setter and G.D. Sontheimer, *Memorial Stones*, Dharwad, 1982) these monuments have been studied in respect of their location, numbers, chronology and their inscriptional contents providing thereby new dimensions to the study of the problem.

Bana provides a vivid description of the burning of the queen Yashomati, the wife of King Prabhakarvardhana of Thanesar (in *c.* 604 A.D.) on the banks of the river Sarasvati. In her reply to the persuasions of her dear son Harsha is reflected the ideal of a true *kshatrani*, the bounden duty of a royal widow. Thus, she said to Harsha:[51]

> I am the lady of a great house ... one
> whose virtue is her dower. Have you
> forgotten that I am the lioness mate
> of a great spirit, who like a lion has
> his delight in hundred battles? I cannot
> endure, like the widowed Rati, to make
> unavailing lamentations for a burnt husband.
> Not in the body, dear son, but in
> glory of loyal widows, I abide on earth.

Although Harsha could not persuade his mother from performing sati, he succeeded in saving his sister Rajyashri, the widowed queen of Kanauj, from entering into the fire in the

Vindhya forests.[52] However, in his other work, the *Kadambari*, Bana condemns *anumarana* in a most spirited and well-reasoned passage. Struck with horror by the tendency to eulogise sati, he crusaded against it. Chandrapida in his address to Mahashveta, cites well-known instances of women like Rati, Kunti, Uttara and Duhsala who did not commit self-immolation.[53] Among the commentators on Manu who opposed the practice of sati, Madhatithi stands unparallel. He compares the practice to *Shyenayaga* which a man performed by way of black magic to kill his enemy. He further argues that it is against the law of Dharma (*adharma*) and not conceded by shastras (*ashastriya*). He maintains that it is suicide and is really forbidden to women and that "one should not leave this world before one has finished one's allotted span of life". He even argues that in some situations a widow should be permitted to remarry.[54] That Madhatithi felt so strongly about it while Manu did not even mention it shows the wider prevalence of the practice during the later period.[55]

The practice of sati was opposed also from religious point of view. According to *Mahanirvanatantra* (a Shakta text) "a wife should not be burnt with her dead husband. Every woman is the embodiment of the goddess. That woman who in her delusion ascends the funeral pyre of her husband, shall go to hell".[56] The earlier Kshatriya notion of a widow's continued dwelling with her husband in heaven after immolation seems to have been replaced by the deification of women. In this context the view that this changed attitude might possibly be "due to non-Kshatriya women specially brahmins being encouraged to become sati" needs further examination.

The literary and archaeological sources considered above show that the custom was prevalent by and large among those who held administrative and military positions generally associated with the Kshatriyas or those who were aspiring for such status. It was disapproved by the Shaktas who had a larger popular base. Further, the discovery of the sati stones in the same locality where hero stones commemorating death in course of a battle have been found, confirms that the practice was originally confined to the martial community. Tribal chiefs are also memorialised in hero stones suggesting the impact of the process of Kshatriyaisation which assimilated them into Sanskrit tradition. Incidently it was also the time when new areas were opened for settlement of the caste-based society and encroachment on larger scale into tribal areas were made.[57]

Apararka quoting several authorities (Paithinasi, Angiras and Vyaghrapada) forbids self-immolation to the brahmin widows.[58] According to the *Padmapurana*, sati is not permitted to other castes specially to the Brahmins.[59] There is no evidence to suggest that the practice was imposed by priests or men on unwilling women. The view that Raghunandana, a late author (1520-1570 A.D.), has purposely changed the reading from 'agre' to 'agne' in the Rigvedic passage to find Vedic sanction to the practice of sati does not hold ground. Kane has conclusively shown that the passage in question was not addressed to widows at all.[60] The practice seems to have continued due to the pressure of tradition on the popular mind. It was first confined to the kings and nobles because the lot of the wives of the conquered kings and warriors was most miserable everywhere. To save themselves from being dishonoured women preferred to die on funeral pyre. This was perhaps the reason why the practice of '*jauhar*' was introduced among the Rajputs. From the Kshatriya the practice spread to other classes. Once it took root, learned commentators and digest writers were not found wanting to support it with arguments and promise of reward in the future. Shankha and Angiras promise eternal bliss to the sati along with her husband in heaven even though he may be a criminal.[61] Her act is hailed as purifying all sins not only of her husband, but also of her parents and of course, herself. If she does not follow her husband she is threatened with many successive rebirths.[62] This despite, there is no evidence to suggest that sati was forced on unwilling widows. Apastamba prescribes *prajapatya* penance for one who having first resolved to burn herself on funeral pyre turns back from it at the last moment.[63] The *Rajatarangini* refers to a queen having pretended to have resolved on becoming a sati ultimately regretted the step and turned back (VI.196). The Smritichandrika (1200-1225 A.D.) considers *anvarohana* as inferior to *brahmacharya* (leading a celibate life) for a widow. The extreme view of Angirasa that "for all women there is no other duty except falling into funeral pyre when the husband dies"[64] was made, as correctly pointed out in the *Suddhitattva*, by way of belauding *sahamarana*.[65] Even the *Mitakshara*[66] which makes *anvarohana* "common to all women of all castes from Brahamana to the Chandala" provides restrictions which are also enjoined by all the Smritis and the Brahan-Naradiya Purana on the widows.[67] There is therefore, no evidence to suggest that widows who did not perform sati were coerced into doing it. Epigraphic and literary evidence from various parts of India is not lacking to show that relatives even tried to dissuade the widow from taking the extreme step. However, it cannot be denied that on rare occasions unbearable agony may also have led a woman to follow her husband into death.

The genesis and growth of sati, as suggested by the foregoing survey, did not follow a universal pattern, it varied in respect of time and space. To make the picture complete the investigation also needs to be extended to the medieval and modern periods. However, it is now possible to indicate several stages it might have followed in course of its growth during the early periods of Indian history.

It originated at some period of time before the composition of the Rigveda wherein it is referred to as a tradition of hoary antiquity. The custom prevailed in a number of civilisations of the ancient world and might probably have prevailed among the indigenous tribes with whom the Aryans assimilated in course of their expansion. The Aryans, who badly needed men for their armed forces did not sanction the burning of the widows but did allow it to remain merely as the symbol of the tradition of bygone age. The early Dharmasutras do not mention sati. This may possibly be explained as due to the prevalence of the practice of *niyoga* (cohabitation), also a relic of the past, alluded to in the Vedas and also approved by the Dharmasutras though with reservations. The Buddhist and Jaina texts do not show any awareness of the rite of sati. The condition of widows was much better under these two religious systems, life had a meaning for them and hence they were not anxious to end it prematurely. The view that sati came into vogue possibly as a reaction to the socio-religious movements cannot be accepted in the absence of evidence to support it. Several Jaina sati memorials from Rajasthan suggest that the practice was also adopted by the Jains at a later stage. The progressive trends in Indian philosophical and religious thought too remained mainly concerned with metaphysical questions and did not provide any answer to the social problems of the day. *Manusmriti* is silent on sati, recommends a pure life on the part of the widow and in special circumstances allows *niyoga* which it disapproves later. *Yajnavalkyasmriti*, a near contemporary text, *Vishnudharmasutra* and Katyayanasmriti also disapprove the practice of *niyoga* although the right of inheritance to widow is approved by them. The gradual discontinuance of *niyoga* and the appearance of sati within the same time bracket does not seem to be a mere coincidence. Its historical significance needs to be fully understood. It may also be noted that from 4th century B.C. to 5th century A.D. (i.e., for more than eight hundred years) the instances of sati are rare.

Enforced widowhood with stress on chastity as a alternative to sati which the texts recommend becomes meaningful if understood in its relation to the notion of control of sexuality in a patriarchal society. A life of purity for a widow of advanced age and nurtured in Indian tradition would not be difficult to follow but for child-widows or those of very tender age the situation would become intolerable. The excessive sufferings to which she was forced by the orthodox section of the society might possibly have led them to prefer the second alternative or perhaps "chastity was not found sufficient guarantee and hence demand for ultimate sacrifice" was made.[68] It may be remembered that even in modern times tremendous efforts were required to be made by social reformers in their task of the emancipation of the Indian widows. It may also be noted that enforced widowhood is not to be found in matriarchal society.

The period from 500 A.D. to 1200 A.D. is crucial for the study of the growth of sati. It finds mention in a variety of sources – secular literature, commentaries on Smritis, Puranas, the accounts of foreign travellers, some of the sectarian texts, inscriptions and last but not the least, 'memorial stones' which add a new dimension to the study of the problem.

The evidence so far considered leaves no doubt that the sati was largely followed by the Kshatriyas. From them it spread to the tribal areas which came under their occupation. The practice was not approved for brahmins in the beginning. But there seems no evidence to suggest the imposition during that period. Confined to kings and warriors it was preferred by the conquered people to save their women from dishonour. It was later approved for other classes although with restrictions and justification found on the promise of reward and penance to those who withdrew. It was primarily an upper-class custom and there seems very little evidence to suggest that the lower-classes had taken to it largely.[69] The role of women in economic production needs to be taken into account before any such generalisation is made. The women of upper-classes had practically no role to play as compared to the lower-classes who were an integral part of the productive process. In the upper-classes women were looked upon as unnecessary burden, they had right to inheritance and hence by observing the practice of sati the family stood to gain.[70] In a recent study,[71] the law of inheritance (*Dayabhaga*) is cited to explain the large number of satis in Bengal. If so, it may be asked how could the lower-classes be concerned with it, since they had very little to inherit. The *Dayabhaga* was composed by Jimutavahana sometime in the middle of the 12th century A.D. Widow burning reached large proportions in Bengal during the early part of the century, immediately preceding its abolition. Unless it is established that the *Dayabhaga* factor continuously worked ever since it was written, it cannot be maintained as the major factor for the larger prevalence of the practice in Bengal.

The problem of the burning of widows, like that of the dowry or untouchability, is a national problem and requires to be combatted at that level. If past is any clue to the future it can be said that legislative measures and public debates have failed to provide any permanent solution to this problem. One is shocked to find a section of public opinion defending this inhuman practice on grounds of the honour of a particular community or its opposition as amounting to interference in religious practices of the people. Perhaps, somewhere beneath the very contradictions of the Indian ethos lies the answer in explaining why a great freedom fighter like Lokamanya Tilak, stands in opposition even to rational attempts at social and religious reforms and why Gandhiji, a great champion of the oppressed classes and of the emancipation of Indian women, suggests 'spiritual corrective' and 'regeneration of individual' instead of a collective action for 'effective change in the society.' It is no wonder that a large section of the Indian people still finds itself so much bound to the traditions which have not only lost all purpose but have been a major ingredient in the retardation of our cultural growth.

Notes

1. H.H. Wilson, *Miscellaneous Essays and Lectures on the Religions of the Hindus* (ed.) Reinhold Rost, Vol.II; H.T. Colebrooke, *Miscellaneous Essays*, 2 Vols., Madras 1872.
2. C.H. Philips (ed.) *The Correspondence of Lord William Cayendish Bentinck*, Oxford, 1977; V.N. Datta, *Sati: Widow Burning in India*, Delhi, 1988, pp.19-70 for details on British policy on 'Sutee'.
3. C.H. Philips, *op.cit.*, I, pp.335-45, 360-62.

4. Elphinstone's Minute (1823), R.D. Choksey, *Mountstuart Elphinstone: The Indian Years* (1796-1827), Bombay, 1971. pp.429-31; see also Elphinstone's *History of India*, Allahabad, 1968, pp.187-88, 'Manners and Character' of the Hindus.
5. C.H. Philips, *op.cit.*
6. V.N. Datta, *op.cit.*; Edward Thompson, *Sutee*, London, 1928; William Jones, *A Collection of Facts and Opinions Relative to the Burning of Widows*, Birmingham, 1816; G.G. Agarkar, *Sudharaka*, 26.9.1892.
7. P.V. Kane, *History of Dharmashastra*, Vol.II, Part-I, Poona, 1974, pp.624-36. Also see Romila Thapar's article, "In History" *Seminar*, February 1988, pp.14-19 for a comprehensive study of the problem in recent times.
8. For the controversy between Radhakanta Deb and H.H. Wilson see latter's *Essays* (*op.cit.*, pp.293-309); Kane, *op.cit.*, p.625, fn.1462.
9. Rammohun Roy, "A Conference between an advocate for and an opponent of the practice of Burning Widows alive", 1818; "A Second Conference between an advocate and opponent of the practice of Burning Widows alive", 1820; J.K. Majumdar (ed.) *Raja Ram Mohan Roy and Progressive Movements in India*, Calcutta, 1898; Ram Prasad Chanda and J.K. Majumdar, *Raja Ram Mohan Roy: Letters and Documents*, Delhi, 1987.
10. *Rigveda*, X.18.8.8; *Athrvaveda*, XII.2.31, XVIII, 3.57.
11. *Atharva*, 18.3.1 and *Tai-Ar*. VI.1.
12. *Brihad-devata*, VII.13; *Ashvalayana Grhyasutra*, IV.6.11-12; 2.16-18; *Baudhayana Pitrmedhasutra*, I 8.1-2,7.
13. *Rigvidhana*, III.8.4 (ed. by Meyer) as quoted by Kane, *op.cit.*, p.618.
14. Kane, *op.cit.*, p.619.
15. *Ibid.*
16. *Ibid.*
17. *Ibid.*, p.625.
18. Edward Balfour, *Cyclopaedia of India*, London, 1885; Schrader "Prehistoric Antiquities of the Aryan People", Eng. Tr.1890; Westermarck "Origin and Development of Moral Ideas", 1906; Kane, *op.cit.*, p.625.
19. In archaeological investigations the term 'Sati-burial' was first used by Gordon Child (*New Light on the Most Ancient East*; 1956, p.149). This has been adopted by S.R. Rao to explain joint-burials at Lothal (*Lothal and Indus Civilization*, Bombay, 1973, p.159), a suggestion which appears to H.D. Sankalia as a 'pure anachronism' for the very spirit behind the Sati practice might be totally absent in the Lothal burial (*The Prehistory and Protohistory of India and Pakistan*, Poona, 1974, p.375).
20. Wilson, *op.cit.*, pp.306-07.

21. Yaska, *Nirukta*, III.15; *Munismrti*, IX,59-61, Medhatithi on Manu IX.66; Visvarupa on *Yaj.* I.68.
22. *Gautama Dharmasutra*, 18.4-14; *Vas.Dh.S.* 17, 56-65; *Bau.Dh.S.* 2.17; Kautilya, *Arthasastra*, I.17, III.6; *Narada, Stripumsa* 84-85.
23. *Ap.Dh.S.* II.10.27. 5-7; Manu IX.64-68; *Brhaspati* as quoted by Apararka, for detailed discussion see Kane, *op.cit.*, pp.599-607.
24. *Mitakshara* on *Yaj.*III.117 also see Apararka.
25. *Brahmapurana* as quoted by Apararka.
26. *Mahabharata*, Adi.Chaps.64, 95, 103-105, 120-23, 177; Anushasana, Chaps.44, 52-53; Santi, 72.12; Winternitz's paper "Notes on the Mahabharata" in *J.R.A.S.* 1897, pp.716-732, for "Niyoga in the great epic" (Kane, *op.cit.*, p.604); Adi. 85, 65, 125.29; Virat, 23.8; Mausala, 7.18, 73-74 for *Sati* in the Mahabharata (Kane, *op.cit.*, p.626).
27. Yaska on Rig.I 124.7; Kane, *op.cit.*, p.581.
28. Kane *op.cit.*, p.582.
29. *Ibid.*
30. Indra, *The Status of Women in Ancient India*, Benaras, 1955, p.296.
31. *Ibid.*, pp.207-08.
32. *Mahavagga Sutta*, VII; *Milindapanha*, IV-4-42, Indra, *op.cit.*, p.189.
33. *Kalpa Sutta*, VII; Indra, *op.cit.*, p.255.
34. *Uttaradhyayana Sutra*, II, IV-20.
35. *Bhadrabahu Samhita, Vardhamananiti* and *Arhanniti* as quoted by Indra, *op.cit.*, pp.264-67.
36. Romila Thapar, *Seminar*, February 1988, p.16.
37. Kane, *op.cit.*, p.443.
38. *Sullayagga*: 18, 21; *Tevigga Sutta*, 33 and *Samyutta Nikaya*, I, 24 as quoted by Indra *op.cit.*, pp.188-89, 191.
39. Romila Thapar, *op.cit.*, p.17.
40. *Ratnakaranda Sravakachara*, Verse 122.
41. *Reality*, Canto VII, Sutra 22 (Sarvarthasiddhi Commentary, Eng.Tr. S.A. Jain, Calcutta, 1960; Justice T.K. Tukol, *Sallekhana is not Suicide*, Ahmedabad, 1976).
42. Govinda Agrawal, "Sati Pratha: Eka Adyayana Aur Vivechana" in *Indological Studies* (ed. Devendra Handa), Delhi, 1987, p.414; Agarchand Bhawarlal Nahata, Bikaner Jaina Lekha Samgraha.
43. K. Antonova, G. Bongard-Levin, G. Kotovsky, *A History of India*, Moscow, 1979, I, pp.113-14, 154.
44. Kane, *op.cit.*, p.603.
45. *Vishnu Dh.S.* 25.14 quoted by the *Mitakshara*.
46. McCrindle, *Ancient India as described in Classical Literature*, p.38. It would be difficult to agree with Thapar's equation of the Kathaioi or

Cathaeans with Khatriya or Khattiya (*op.cit.*, p.15). Possibly they were connected with the Katha people (H.C. Raychaudhuri, *Political History of Ancient India*, Calcutta, 1953, pp.250-51, also fn.1-4) associated with composition of some of the Brahmanical texts. If accepted it would mean that the earliest historical evidence pertaining to the practice of Sati comes from the Brahmanical class. Interestingly the Greek writers have also mentioned a people known as Xathroi-Kshatri (Raychaudhuri, *op.cit.*, p.257).

47. E.J. Rapson (ed.), *Cambridge History of India: Ancient India*, Vol.I, p.415.
48. J. Fleet, CII (*Gupta Inscriptions*), p.91.
49. Elliot and Dawson, *The History of India as told by its own Historians*, Vol.I, Chap.I; *Alberuni's India* (ed.) Edward C. Sachau, Indian edn.1964, II, p.155.
    The rite of Sati is also referred to in the *Ramayana*, the *Hitopadesha*, the *Kathasaritsagara*, the *Kavyamimansa*, the *Smrtichandrika* of Devannabhata, the *Prthvirajaraso*, the later Puranic literature and the *Mahanirvana-tantra*.
50. Kane, *op.cit.*, p.629 for a brief account of the epigraphic evidence on the Sati.
51. The *Harshacharita* of Bana (Tr. E.B. Cowell and F.W. Thomas) pp.148, 154-55.
52. *Ibid.*, pp.248-50.
53. *Kadambari* of Bana (ed.) Kane, Purvabhaga, para 177.
54. Medhatithi on Manu, V, 156-57; Kane, *op.cit.*, pp.631-32.
55. Romila Thapar, op.cit., p.15.
56. As quoted by Thapar, p.17.
57. *Ibid.*, p.16.
58. Kane, *op.cit.*, p.627.
59. *Padmapurana* as quoted by Thapar.
60. Kane, *op.cit.*, p.634.
61. *Ibid.*, p.631.
62. Quoted by *Mitakshara* on Yaj.I.86.
63. As quoted by Aparaka and *Suddhitatva*; Kane, *op.cit.*, p.633.
64. Kane, *op.cit.*, Angirasa as quoted by Aparaka.
65. *Ibid.*
66. *Mitakshara* on Yaj.I.86.
67. Kane, *op.cit.*, p.633.
68. K.N.Panikkar, Review Article, *Seminar*, February 1988, p.45.
69. V.N. Datta, *op.cit.*
70. Panikkar, *op.cit.*
71. V.N. Datta, *op.cit.*

5

Sources of the History of Ayodhya (*c.* 606-1206 A.D.): A Historiographical Study

The ancient town of Ayodhya has become in recent years a subject of fierce controversy among politicians, religious leaders and also academicians. Its impact, felt throughout the country, was even much deeper than what the historicity and date of the Mahabharata (1975) or the Daurala Sati event could probably make. The twin issues of the Babri Masjid and Ramajanmabhumi over which volumes of literature was produced during the last few years only reveal the complex nature of the problem which has completely changed the very life of the town. It would, therefore, be in the fitness of things first to make a thorough analyses of the source material so that the growth of the town through the ages is properly understood. An attempt would be made here at a historiographical study of the sources of the history of Ayodhya from *c.* 606 A.D. to 1206 A.D. For a comparative view, statistical data, whatever available, shall be pressed into service for the first time.

We have purposely taken *c.* 606 A.D. as our starting point because it was the year when King Harshavardhana shifted his capital to Kanauj. Ayodhya which was not very far, formed a part of the kingdom of Kanauj as is suggested by the discovery of Pratapashila and Shiladitya coins from Bhitaura (Faizabad) and Ayodhya,[1] and the evidence of the Chinese pilgrim, Yuan Chwang who visited Ayodhya during Harsha's reign but does not make any specific mention of the ruler of that town.[2] Further, it may be pointed out that the coins of Maukhari Ishanavarman, Sarvavarman and Avantivarman have also been discovered from the said places where the Vardhana coins were found[3] which makes it all the more probable that they were the rulers of Ayodhya as well, a position which later passed on to Harsha in course of succession. R.G. Basak has very rightly designated them as the 'Maukharis of Ayodhya'.[4]

When on his onward journey from Ayodhya the Chinese pilgrim proceeded down the Ganga with about eighty other fellow passengers on board a ship, robbers selected him as an offering to the goddess Durga and it was fortunately through the intercession of nature that he escaped.[5] This is an important passage throwing interesting light on the condition prevailing in the neighbourhood of Ayodhya where non-Buddhists must have been numerous, a situation which stands in sharp contrast to that of the latter place (Ayodhya), where the pilgrim found only ten Deva temples and few non-Buddhists while the number of Buddhists monasteries was about one hundred.[6]

The Chinese pilgrim adds the following details on Ayodhya:[6a]

> A-yu-te was about 1,000 *li* in circuit, and the capital was above twenty *li*. The country yielded good crops, was luxuriant in fruit and flower, and had a genial climate. The people had agreeable ways, were fond of good works, and devoted to practical learning.
>
> (In the) Buddhist monasteries, (of Ayodhya) there were more than 3,000 Brethren who were students of both 'Vehicles'...

(Among the Buddhist remains of the town, special mention is made of Sangharamas associated with Asanga and Vasubandhu and a sacred *stupa* built by Ashokaraja).

The observations of the Chinese may generally be taken as a sad commentary on the attitude of the non-Buddhists towards the followers of Buddhism and particularly a foreigner who was initiated in that faith. The culprits may not necessarily be robbers as described by the Chinese pilgrim but may be some of those of the orthodox Brahmanical section who were later worsted in the Kanauj assembly before the powerful argumentation skill of the Chinese, and who had possible links with the plot to assassinate the pilgrim and his patron, King Harsha. Further, as the pilgrim relates, some of their leaders were put to death and about five hundred Brahmins were arrested and exiled.[7]

It would indeed be rewarding if the observations of the Chinese pilgrim on Ayodhya are compared with those of his on Kanauj, Prayaga and Varanasi. At all these places he found the non-Buddhists in great numbers. The number of monasteries at Kanauj was hundred, it came down to two at Prayaga while it was thirty at Varanasi whose inhabitants cared very little for Buddhism.[8] In view of the above it would not be unreasonable to suggest that during the times of Harsha, Buddhist influence remained predominant in Ayodhya. Possible Maukhari inclination towards that faith might have also added towards this end.

In the absence of indigenous sources of information one has to depend on the Chinese and Tibetan account for a glimpse of the history of Kanauj (of which Ayodhya formed a part) immediately after Harsha's death in the year 647 or 648 A.D.[9] It is nothing but a sad tale of confusion and anarchy. We hear for the first time the name of Arunashva or Arjuna, a minister who usurped the throne.[10] The epigraphic sources provide 'varman-ending' names of a few princes such as Suchandravaman,

Bhogavarman and Manorathavarman, suggesting their possible Maukhari connection,[11] while *Kuvalayamala*, a Jaina work of the 8th century, mentions Drdhavarman probably a ruler of Ayodhya.[12] There is no doubt that Ayodhya was closely linked with the fortunes of the kingdom of Kanauj of which it formed a part, but on the basis of such meagre evidence it may not be possible to establish any link of the above princes with either Kanauj or Ayodhya or the Maukharis who were ruling over those places.

Ayodhya again finds mention in connection with the conquest of Yashovarman, the ruler of Kanauj. According to *Gaudavaho*, the king marched to the site of Ayodhya, the city of Harishchandra where he built a temple.[13] After Yashovarman during the later half of the 8th century A.D., we hear of three rulers – Chakrayudha, Indrayudha and Vajrayudha, who ruled over the kingdom of Kanauj. We do not know anything regarding their connection with Yashovarman or the place they originally belonged to.[14] Could it be Ayodhya? Possibility may not be altogether ruled out in view of the close relationship between that place and Kanauj ever since the time of the Maukharis. It would be difficult to connect the Ayudhas with Ayodhya on linguistic grounds alone. Ayodhya was in all probability included in the empire of Kanauj under the Pratiharas which extended as far as Bihar and northern Bengal in the east. This receives some support from the recovery of Adi-varaha types of coins from Hatila, near Faizabad.[15] When did Ayodhya fell apart from the Pratihara dominion, we do not know. It again figures with the rise of the Gahadavalas who held themselves specially responsible for protecting that sacred city along with Varanasi, Kanyakubja and Indrasthaniya. The Chandravati inscription of the time of Chandradeva makes special mention of this historic role befallen on the Gahadavalas in view of repeated Turkish onslaughts in their region.[16] The greater portion of the

Gahadavala dominions included Kanauj, Badaun, Jaunpur, Chunar, Rohtasgarh, Varanasi and Ayodhya which latter seems to have remained outside the sphere of political influence of the Turks[17] and continued to be so for quite sometime as is gathered from the evidence of the *Tabaqat-i-Nasiri*.[18]

That Ayodhya too, like other parts of the kingdom of Kanauj, was in constant danger of the Turk attack becomes evident also from the system of revenue which imposed a new tax known as *Turushka danda* referred to in about thirty-one of the Gahadavala inscriptions covering all the reigns from Chandradeva to Vijayachandra and was collected from all parts of the kingdom of Kanauj.[19] This tax was later discontinued from the reign of Jayachandra, possibly because of the fact that Chahamanas who were already in possession of Delhi, completely freed northern India from the Turk menace and as very aptly put in the Delhi Sivalik inscription, Aryavarta once again became the abode of the Aryans.[20]

There has been some difference of opinion regarding the interpretation of the term *Turushkadanda* but Smith, Ghoshal, Rangaswami Aiyangar and Altekar have given convincing arguments in favour of taking it as a contribution from the people to ward off the Turushkas.[21]

It is surprising that Al-Beruni who visited India in the train of Mahmud of Ghazni, mentions Ayodhya, its location and distance from other specific places but does not provide any detail of the conditions that prevailed there.[22] Similarly, no less puzzling is the fact that Rajashekhara, the court poet of the Pratiharas and an elderly contemporary of Al-Beruni, does not give any description of the town. Although geography seems to be a subject of the poet's special interest (as is gathered from the geographical data incorporated in his works – the *Kavyamimansa, Balaramayana* and the *Bhuvana Kosha*) but hardly does he give any information on the town which was so near to Kanauj, the capital city where he lived under the royal patronage. One is all the more surprised to find that even in his drama on the Ramayana theme; the poet does not think it necessary to describe Ayodhya wherever it would have been quite appropriate for him to do.[23] Similarly, inclusion of many sacred places in the Gahadavala dominion might have inspired Lakshmidhara, their court poet, to devote a whole section of his book *Krtyakalpataru* to *Tirthavivechana* but it is to be regretted that the author relied exclusively on the Puranic literature and deprived us of a contemporary account, at least of the four *tirthas* which were specially under the protection of the Gahadavala monarchs.

After the defeat of Jayachandra in the battle of Chandwar (1193 A.D.), most of the Gahadavala territory passed on to the new masters. Banares was destroyed. Nearly one thousand of its temples were pulled down and mosques were raised on their foundations.[24] Similar must have been the fate of Ayodhya. The *Tabaqat-i-Nasiri* mentions not only Kanauj but also Badaun and Ayodhya amongst the conquests of Iltutmish,[25] the last was conferred in the year 623 on Malik Nasir-ud-Din, his eldest son. The *Tabaqat-i-Nasiri* provides a brief description of the disaster which befell the town. It states:[26]

> In that country (Ayodhya), the prince (Malik Nasir-ud-Din) performed numerous commendable actions, and carried on holy war, as by the tenets of the faith enjoined, so that his praise for manliness and boldness became diffused throughout the area of Hindustan. The accursed Bartu (the local ruler of Ayodhya) beneath whose sword about a hundred and twenty thousand Musalmans had attained martyrdom, he overthrew and sent to Hell; and the refractory infidels who were in different parts of the country of Awadh, he reduced and overcame, and brought a considerable number under obedience.

This is an important passage and needs to be commented upon. First, it refers to the oppressive measures of the new administration which must have included the destruction of temples as was done at several other places. This need not surprise us because some of the early Sultans of the Delhi were iconoclasts, and the *Tabaqat-i-Nasiri* mentions two such accomplishments of Iltutmish – the demolition of an idol temple at Bhilsa (which took three-hundred years in building) and the destruction of the Mahankala temple at Ujjain.[27] The *Tabaqat-i-Nasiri* gives the name of the local ruler of Ayodhya as Bartu who seems to have offered a stiff resistance to the advance of the Turk invaders and hence, was severely punished. A fragmentary stone inscription found in Nagod State, Central India, implies the existence of one Mahasamanta Barahadeva, a powerful feudatory of the Gahadavalas, probably ruling over Kanauj during Jayachandra's reign who was ultimately overthrown by Iltutmish.[28] Could he be the same mentioned in the *Tabaqat-i-Nasiri* as Bartu, a chief of Ayodhya? This chief has been regarded by scholars as either some descendant of the Gahadavala dynasty or one of their feudatories.[29]

With the destruction of numerous temples, of which some might have been fine specimen of architecture and sculpture of the early-medieval times, also perished valuable material for the study of religious history of Ayodhya. The *Tabaqat-i-Nasiri* passage does not make direct mention of temple destruction at Ayodhya but that seems implied when reference to 'holy war' and 'refractory infidels' is made. It appears that the city must have gone through such critical times earlier also. This explains why after Yuan Chwang, no specific mention of Ayodhya is made either by Arab historians or by contemporary Indian writers. The Puranic account is mostly traditional and has hardly any bearing on the contemporary times. Details of art remains from Ayodhya of the early medieval period are also not very much known. Similarly, Buddhist remains of

Ayodhya which had been an important centre of Buddhism when Yuan Chwang visited it, need to be carefully studied.[30] It may be that during the later-Pratihara period Ayodhya was also subjected to Ghaznavid attacks. Sultan Masud who succeeded Sultan Mahmud, led his army several times into Hindustan and carried on holy wars as by law enjoined. But more relevant is the career of his general Ahmad Niyaltagin who crossed the river Ganges and went down to the left bank and "arrived at Benares to which place never had a Muhammadan army reached before (1033 A.D.)".[31] It is to be noted that in course of his march through the Gangetic Valley, the general met with no resistance and even Banares was left to the tender mercies of the invader who thoroughly destroyed it.[32] That there was no competent government in Antarvedi and Varanasi region to check the Turk menace and remove the distress of the people becomes evident from the statement of Habib-us-Siyar regarding the expedition of Sultan Ibrahim (1059-1099 A.D.) in this region.[33] The situation changed only when Chandradeva Gahadavala seized power and put an end to the suffering of the people. It is to be remembered that the king, in one of his inscriptions, claims to have taken under his protection several sacred places which includes Ayodhya. Yet another expedition was sent during the times of Masud (III)-ibn-Ibrahim (*c.* 1099-1115 A.D.). Hajib Tugh-tigin who was in-charge of the venture, crossed the river Ganges "in order to carry on holy war in Hindustan and penetrate to places to which no man has reached so far with army before".[34] The contemporary poet Salman in his *Diwan* gives more details of the expedition specially the capture of Malhi, the ruler of Kanauj. The latter has been identified with Madanapala Gahadavala who was released due to the efforts of his son Govindachandra, the valiant crown-prince of the dynasty.[35]

It would thus become sufficiently clear that from the later-Pratihara times Antarvedi (which included Ayodhya) was subjected to Turk raids several times and consequently peace and stability completely departed from the region. Although there is no direct mention of Ayodhya in this regard yet it was so near to Kanauj, the capital city, that its fate was bound to be affected by what happened at the latter place. That the place does not find specific mention in contemporary writings also suggests the decline of the town. Several religious structures of Ayodhya might possibly have been destroyed even before the establishment of Sultanate; whatever remained was demolished soon thereafter. The Gahadavalas did try to restore order and protect Ayodhya along with other holy places under their jurisdiction; the imposition of a new tax *Turushka Danda* by the Gahadavalas needs to be understood in this context. With the fall of the Gahadavalas, Ayodhya lost its protectors for a long time to come. During the Sultanate, when policy of religious persecution was persistently followed, the possibility of construction of new Hindu religious complexes at Ayodhya may be said to be remote. There is therefore, no reasonable ground to contend that a temple remained at Ayodhya till the time of Babur or that after the demolition of such a structure a mosque was built over that site. The entire place must have been a town in ruins and there is nothing surprising that material of the old ruined structures which was so easily available, was used in the construction of the Babri Mosque. This has been the case at several other places where temple destruction was carried out.

An analytical study of the sources of the history of Ayodhya (from 606 to 1206 A.D.) thus shows that Buddhism remained dominant over there under the Maukharis and the Vardhanas. Since then, not much is known of its history till the rise of the Gahaḍavalas who took it under their special care and protection. The town seems to have passed through a period of decline as there is no specific mention of the town either in the accounts of Arab writers or in the contemporary Indian works.

It must have been subjected to the foreign inroads several times. It was finally conquered by Iltutmish. The contemporary Arab writers, although speak of a 'holy war' or 'destruction of infidels', they do not particularly mention demolition of temples at Ayodhya as is the case with a number of holy places which met with that fate. This removes all possibility of the existence of any temple worthy of mention at that site, not to speak of any dedicated to the worship of Rama. The basic question which emerges out of the discussion in not of fixing the responsibility of demolition of any particular religious structure or of restoring it to its former position but to know *what it is* that allows the followers of a particular faith to demolish religious complexes of others? *What is it* which leads them to declare 'holy war' or 'destruction of infidels' (even in this 20th century!) or for that matter, of Mlechchhas or the aliens who were specially ordained not to enter any Hindu temple (*Arya Dharmetaranam pravesho nishidhah*). There may be instances of pious individuals who raised their voice against such irreligious and irrational measures but were there persons who could collectively take a stand so as to prevent the rulers from following such a disastrous course? In the answers to these fundamental questions lies the solution to the Ramajanmabhumi/Babri Masjid issue which has submerged this town of high antiquity into the deep waters of sufferings and misery in recent times.

Notes

1. *JRAS.*, 1906, p.943-50; 1909, pp.446-48; *ASIR*, IX, p.27.
2. Thomas Watters, *On Yuan Chwang's Travels in India*, Delhi, 1961, Vol.I, pp.354-55; Samuel Beal, *Buddhist Records of the Western World*, London, 1884, I, p.225.
3. *JRAS, op.cit., ASIR, op.cit.*
4. *Ibid.*, 1889, p.270.

5. Shaman Hwui Li, *The Life of Hiuen Tsiang*, Academica Asiatica, Delhi, 1973, Book III, p.86-90.
6. Watters, *op.cit.; Beal, op.cit.*

6a *Ibid.*

7. *Life*, pp.179-80; Beal, *op.cit.*, I, pp.219-21 (for more details).
8. For a comparative study with the position of Buddhism at Kanauj, Prayaga and Varanasi see Watters, I, pp.340, 361; II, p.47; Beal, I, pp.207, 230; II, pp.44-5.
9. R.S. Tripathi, *History of Kanauj*, Benares, 1937, pp.188-90; *JASB.*, 1837, pp.69-70.
10. *Ibid.*
11. Buddha Prakash, *Aspects of Indian History and Civilization*, Agra, 1965, pp.101-102, 116.
12. *Kuvalayamala* of Udyotana Suri, (ed.) A.N. Upadhye (Singhi Jaina Granthamala), p.180.
13. *Gaudavaho*, (ed.) S.P. Pandit, "Introduction"; Buddha Prakash, *op.cit.*, p.103; Tripathi, *op.cit.*, p.199.
14. Tripathi, *op.cit.*, pp.212-18.
15. B.N. Puri, *The History of the Gurjara-Pratiharas*, Bombay, 1957, p.153; *ASR*, I, p.329.
16. Roma Niyogi, *The History of the Gahadavala Dynasty*, Calcutta, 1959, p.46.
17. *Epigraphia Indica*, XIV, pp.193-96; *Indian Historical Quarterly*, 1949, pp.31-37; Niyogi, *op.cit.*, p.127.
18. *Tabaqat-i-Nasiri*, English Tr. by Raverty, I, 1970, pp.628-29.
19. Niyogi, *op.cit.*, pp.176-81 (for detailed discussion).
20. *Indian Antiquary*, XIX, pp.215-19.
21. Niyogi, *op.cit.*; Krtyakalpataru, (ed.), K.A. Rangaswami, Baroda, Rajadharmakanda, "Introduction", p.53, fn.1; Smith, *Early History of India*, p.400, fn.1; Ghoshal, *Hindu Revenue System*, p.263; Altekar, *State and Government in Ancient India*, p.277.
22. Edward Sachau, *Al-Beruni's India*, Delhi, 1964, I, p.200.
23. Rajashekhara, *Balaramayana*, X, Verse 96. The poet devotes only one verse for the description of Ayodhya:
   राज्ञां रवें: प्रभवतां कुलराजधानीमालोकयामरपुरी प्रतिमामयोध्याम्।
   वार्भि: शरच्छशिकर द्युतिभि: सरय्वां या पूर्वपार्थिव यशोभिरिवावभाति ॥26॥
   (ed. Gangasagar Rai, p.368, Varanasi, 1984)
24. Elliot and Dawson, *History of India as Told by Her Own Historians*, II, pp.226 ff; *Tarikh-i-Firishta*, Eng. Trans. Briggs, London, 1829, I, p.179.
25. *Tabaqat-i-Nasiri*, p.627.
26. *Ibid.*, pp.628-29.

27. *Ibid.*, pp.621-22.
28. *Epigraphia Indica*, XXIII, pp.186-89.
29. Niyogi, *op.cit.*, p.119.
30. This point figured in the observations of some of the historians in the recent controversy.
31. *Tabaqat-i-Nasiri*, *op.cit.*, pp.93-5; Elliot and Dawson, *op.cit.*, II, pp.123-24; *Cambridge History of India,* III, pp.29-30.
32. Niyogi, *op.cit.*, pp.13-14.
33. Elliot and Dawson, IV, pp.205, 523-4.
34. H.C. Ray, *Dynastic History of Northern India*, Calcutta, 1931-36, I, p.514.
35. Niyogi, *op.cit.*, p.59.

6

Literary Sources on the Historical Geography of Ancient Panjab

The ancient Panjab denotes three geographical terms mentioned in early Indian literature. Vedic *Saptasindhu* (i.e., land of seven rivers) is the same occurring in *Avesta as Hapta Hindu; Panchanada* is found in the epics while it is known as *Uttarapatha* to the Brahmanical and Buddhist literature. Of these, *Panchanada* (used for indicating the area through which the five rivers of Panjab, namely, Jhelum, Chenab, Ravi, Beas and Sutlej flowed or their meeting point before they joined the Indus) comes closer to the word Panjab, a compound of two Persian words - *Punj* (five) and *ab* (water), also signifying the land of the five rivers or waters. The earliest use of 'Panjab' occurs in the writings of Ibn-Battutah, an Arab writer who visited India in the 14th century. The term, if applied to the present state of Panjab, would certainly be a misnomer, for since the partition of India in 1947, only two rivers, Sutlej and Beas, lie within its territory.[1]

How was this region known before the advent of the Aryans? What were its geographical and administrative divisions? No precise answers could be given to these questions in the absence of the decipherment of the Indus Valley script and any other contemporary written record. But from the excavations which have been conducted in the region since 1921 a number of pre-historic and proto-historic sites have come to light, although their identification with ancient place-names found in literature is extremely difficult.

The Vedic Literature

The *Rigveda* is the earliest written record providing geographical details of the Panjab (the earliest Aryan settlement in India), its rivers, localities and the tribes who lived there. The Rigvedic *Saptasindhu* denoted the wide area watered by seven rivers, i.e., Sindhu (Indus), its five tributaries and the Sarasvati. In one hymn Sindhu is explicitly called 'mother' of the rivers and the Sarasvati as 'the seventh'.[2] The Rigveda provides the following details of the geography of the Panjab[3]:

(i) *Rivers*: Sindhu (Indus), Vitasta (Jhelum), Asikni (Chenab), Parushni (Ravi), Vipas (Beas), Shutudri (Sutlej), Sushoma (Sohan), Arjikiya (a small river), Hariyupiya (Harappa? or a river), Sarasvati, Drshadvati (Chitang), Apaya (between Sarasvati and Drshadvati).

(ii) *Tribes*: The term 'Panchajanah' (the five people) has been generally equated with the Vedic clans Anu, Yadu, Turvasa, Druhyu and Puru, associated with post-Vedic legend of Yayati and his five sons of the lunar race. The Anus, Druhyus and Turvasa occupied the land between Chenab and Ravi, the Yadus lived in southern Panjab, while the Purus, settled on either side of the Sarasvati, assimilated with the Bharatas (a tribe settled between Sarasvati and the Yamuna) and later formed the famous Kurus.

The *dasharajna* war hymns are a valuable source of information for they not only mention a number of other tribes who participated in it but also give possible indication of the territory they occupied. Of these, the Tritsus occupied the land to the east of Ravi, the Krivis lived on the Sindhu and Chenab, the Bhalanasas, Vishanins, Alinas and Gandharis lived in the extreme north-west, Shivas (Sibis of the later period) may be traced in the Jhang district of Pakistan.

To this list may be added Kekayas (near Jhelum), Madras (Sialkot region), Salvas (on the Yamuna), and Kurukshetra occurring in the later-Vedic texts. Kurukshetra occupied an important place in the geography of ancient Panjab. The line of demarcation between Uttarapatha and Madhyadesha passed through it and hence references to its adjoining areas were made in relation to it. The classification of northern India into Udichya and Prachya made by Panini and later grammarians has been further explained more explicitly in the *Amarakosha* while stating that the river Sarasvati was the dividing line to the north-west of which lay Udichya (which includes the whole of Panjab) and to the south-east of it, the Prachya.[4]

Buddhist Texts

Uttarapatha, the territorial designation used in the Buddhist traditional literature included the whole of ancient Panjab. According to one view it was so named after a trade route which passed from Sravasti (in Kosala) to Takshashila (in Gandhara).[5] However, it seems that in practice Uttarapatha denoted north-western division of India including Kasmira, Gandhara and Kamboja.

The *Anguttara Nikaya* mentions Gandhara and Kamboja among the sixteen *Mahajanapadas* that flourished in the age of the Buddha.[6] This *Janapada* list includes only two names from the Uttarapatha possibly because of the shifting of the centre of political and cultural life to eastern India, a process which had already begun from the later-Vedic period. The *Majjhima* and the *Digha Nikayas* are also acquainted with Gandhara which along with its capital, Taxila finds frequent mention in the Jatakas.[7] The *Mulasaravastivada Vinaya* mentions Kasmira, Bhadrankara (Sakala according to Przyluski), Udumbara (in the Kangra valley) and Rohitaka. The text seems to indicate Buddha's visit to Madra and Sakala and that of the famous physician Jivaka to Taxila, Sakala, Udumbara and Rohitaka.[8]

The *Mahavastu*, *Mahasati-patthana* and *Ratthapala suttas* and the *Kurudhamma Jataka* specially mention Buddha's visit to the Kuru *Janapada*.[9] Buddha's visit to north-western India is also preserved in Sanskrit. Chinese and Tibetan Buddhist texts.[10] The *Jatakas* and the *Atthakatha* mention Madda (Madra) and Sagala (the capital), Sibis and Aritthapura (the capital), Sindhurattha, Sovira (Sauvira), Kamboja and Kekaka (Kekaya).[11] The *Dipavamsa* and *Mahavamsa* while describing the growth of Buddhism during the times of Ashoka mention Majjhantika as the head of Buddhist mission to Kasmira and Gandhara.[12] This finds corroboration in the account of Yuan Chwang, the *Mulasarvastivada Vinaya* and the *Divyavadana*.[13] Ashokan Rock Edicts found at Shahbazgarhi (near Peshawar) and Mansera (in Hazara district) refer to the Kambojas and the Gandharas while his building of several *stupa*s in Uttarapatha finds confirmation in the account of Yuan Chwang[14] and the *Rajatarangini*. On the basis of the evidences cited above it may not be possible to say precisely whether Buddha visited Uttarapatha but it may reasonably be inferred that the region was introduced to Buddhism during the life-time of the Master and that a beginning had been made towards its propagation in the subsequent periods.

Works on Sanskrit Grammar

Panini's *Ashtadhyayi*, a work on Sanskrit grammar composed in *c.* 500 B.C. mentions a number of *janapadas* and some well-known towns of the Panjab. As the author himself belonged to this region (as his name Shalaturiya and Vahika would suggest) his geographical knowledge of the region seems to be direct and hence more authentic, finding substantial confirmation also in the accounts of the classical writers. The geographical data as gleaned from the work of Panini are as follows:[15]

(i) *Janapadas*: Kamboja, Gandhara, Sindhu-Sauvira, Brahmanaka (Brahmanabad in Sindh), Kashmira, Kekaya (Jhelum, Shahpur and Gujarat area), Madra and Ushinara (parts of ancient Vahika), Shaudrayana (on the eastern bank of the Indus), Ambastha (lower course of Chenab), Trigarta (between Ravi, Beas and Sutlej), Salva (included parts of southern Panjab), Udumbara (between Ravi and Beas), Tilakhala (in Kurukshetra region), Urasha (between Sindhu and Jhelum) and Yaudheya (between Sutlej and Yamuna) and Kuru.

(ii) *Towns*: Sarkara (on the Indus), Sankala (Sangalwala in district Jhang), Arishtapura, Phalakapur (Phillor in district Jalandhar), Saubhuta (a town of Kekaya), Saralaka (Sahrala in district Ludhiana), Shalatura (Lahur), Takshashila and Varnava (Bannu in western Panjab).[16]

Panini's geographical knowledge agrees to a great extent with Patanjali, another renowned grammarian who flourished in the second century B.C. In the *Mahabhashya* occur a number of territories of this region which, following his illustrious predecessor, Patanjali includes in Udichya direction. The countries are Kamboja, Kashmira, Gandhara, Kekaya, Salva, Udumbara, Bodha (eastern Panjab), Darvya (between Jhelum and Chenab), Vasati (confluence of Chenab and Sutlej), Vahika (the region between Indus and Sutlej), Brahmanaka, Ushinara, Sibi, Sindhu, Sauvira, Madra, Trigarta and Kuru.

The Epics

The epics, the Ramayana and the Mahabharata are other important literary sources on the historical geography of the region. The earliest strata of both these compositions belong to the Sutra period (i.e., between 700-500 B.C.) but their final editions were completed as late as the early Gupta period.[17] The geographical horizon of these works therefore covers a very wider time-scale of early Indian history.

The Ramayana[18] refers to a number of *janapadas* and some capital towns of Panchanada: Kamboja, Yavana, Shaka, Darada, Harita, Kirata, Barbara, Kekaya, Gandhara, Sindhu, Sauvira, Madraka, Prasthala (the land of Ravi, Beas and Sutlej valleys), Bharata, Kuru, Takshashila and Pushkalavati. But the most important piece of information from our point of view is the description of the route from Ayodhya to Kekaya followed by the couriers and that chosen by Bharata from Girivraja (the capital of Kekaya, modern Girjak or Jalalpur on the bank of Jhelum) to Ayodhya mentioning the territories covered by them. The messengers crossed the Yamuna and passed through Kurujangala, Sharadanda (Chautang), another river, Kulingas, Abhikala, the river Ikshumati (Sarasvati), Vahika (part of Panjab), the mountain Sudaman and the holy Vishnupada on the Vipasa (Beas) and finally reached Kekaya, their destination. The journey thus appears to have followed the route via Panipat, Jind, Sirsa and the Sutlej (somewhere near Fazilka). But the authenticity of the account of Bharata's journey through the region remains doubtful because some of the place-names and rivers mentioned therein are not known to any other literary source. A scholar has recently suggested that in Panjab Bharata probably followed the course starting from Girivraja to Sargoda, Sangla Hills, Lahore, Taran Taran, Kapurthala, Ludhiana (Ailadhana), Bassi, Kataha, Nahan, Majra in Sirmur district and then followed his eastward journey to Ayodhya.[19]

Panjab was known to the Mahabharata[20] as Panchanada (i.e., the land of five rivers) also known as Arattadesha and Vahika. Aratta literally means 'kingless' perhaps indicating the republican character of some of its people, while Vahika denotes traditionally the area around the river Vipasha (Beas; Amritsar and Kapurthala districts) where lived the two *pishachas*, Vahi and Hika who gave their name to the *janapada* and their descendants were hence called Vahikas. The later designation came to be applied in course of time to all the tribes of Panchanada or the Aratta. One of their branches settled at Shakala (Sialkot) was called Jartikas (possibly the ancestors of modern Jats). In the Karnaparva, the people of Panchanada specifically the Madras, the Vahikas and the Arattas are subjected to the abusive attack of Karna in course of his serious arguments with Shalya, the Madra King, who had to act (as was fated) as the former's charioteer. It has been pointed out that Karna's scathing attacks reflect indeed the social and cultural gulf that existed between the eastern orthodoxy on the one hand, and non-conservative element of the composite culture of the land of five rivers, on the other.[21]

The Mahabharata provides an exhaustive list of the *janapadas* and peoples of the Panjab as also the northern and north-western countries who came in contact with them. The *Panchanada janapada*-list included: Gandhara, Sindhu, Sauvira, Madra, Kekaya, Trigarta, Mavellaka, Uluta (Kulu), Kuninda, Kurukshetra, Ushinara, Shibi, Ambastha, Malava, Kshudraka, Yaudheya, Vasati, Vatadhana, Shalva, Bodha, Shudra, Abhira, Gramaniya (on the bank of Indus), Paravatiya (Kangra and Chamba), Kinnara (east of Mandi and Kulu region), Darvas and Abhisara (the people of Punch and Naoshera region, between Jhelum and Chenab) and Kashmira. Of these, the rulers of Gandhara, Sindhu, Sauvira, Madra, Trigarta, Mavellaka and the chiefs of Ushinara, Shibi, Ambastha, Malava, Kshudraka, Vatadhana, Shudra, Abhira, Vasati and Dashtarna participated in the great battle on the Kaurava side. The Panjab rulers on the Pandava side were those of Kekaya, Kuluta, Kulinda and the Yaudheya together with a branch of each of the Ambashthas and the Malavas. Elsewhere in course of Nakula's conquests of western region a number of the above territorial units also find mention along with those (which form parts of Haryana) such as Rohitaka, Bahudhanyaka, Shairishaka, Mahottha and Dasharna, covering almost the whole of ancient Panjab (*Krtsnam panchanadam*)[22]. These references undoubtedly show the contribution of various peoples to the historical and cultural growth of the ancient Panjab.

The Puranas

The Puranas[23] also contain valuable information on historical geography. They follow closely the epics in their geographical data with slight variations in place-names and additions necessitated with the course of time.

Such information is gathered specially from the Kurma *vibhaga* or Bhuvanakosha sections of these works. The Puranas seem to have drawn largely from earlier works including those on astronomy; the Markandeya Purana for instance, borrows expensively from the works of Parashara and Varahamihira.[24] The literary productions of the Gupta and the post-Gupta periods depend largely on Puranic literature for geographical data and therefore, need no special mention. Some of the works of Kalidasa, Rajashekhara's *Balaramayana, Kavyamimansa* and *Bhuvanakosha* and Kalhana's *Rajatarangini* may be cited as examples of this class of literature.

Accounts of Foreign Writers

To the accounts of foreign writers - Greek, Roman, Chinese and Persian, we are indeed very much indebted not only for their corroborative value but also for their keen, perceptive observations providing such details which are otherwise not available in any Indian source. These accounts are of two classes, the narratives of eye witnesses and general description gathered from various sources.

The Classical Accounts[25]

According to the Greek sources Gandhara and Sindhu formed parts of the Persian empire during the sixth and fifth centuries B.C. *Herodotus* (i, 153, 177) informs that the eastern conquests of Cyrus (558-530 B.C.) included Gandaritis (Gandhara). The Persepolis (518-515 B.C.) and Naksh-i-Rustam (515 B.C.); inscriptions of Darius (522-486 B.C.) mention Gandhara and Hindu (Sindhu or Panjab) which then formed the twentieth satrapy of the Persian empire (*Herodotus*, iii, 94). Under Xerxes (486-465 B.C.) the Gandharians and the Indians (comprising the people of Panjab) even fought with the Greeks in Europe. More geographical details of the Panjab are available in the accounts of Alexander's campaigns in the East supplying valuable information on location, population, economy and nature of government of the Indian states coming under their observation. There are, however, some difficulties in the exact location of places because of the changes in the courses of rivers. It would be necessary to get oneself acquainted with the Greek forms of names of the five great eastern tributaries of the Indus which in fact denoted the derivation of the term 'Panjab'. These are: Hydaspes (Jhelum), Acesines (Chenab), Hydraotes (Ravi), Hyphasis or Hypanis (Beas) and Hesidrus (Sutlej). A good account of these rivers of the Panjab is given by Arrian. The observations of the classical writers tell us about territorial units of the Panjab and at some places also about their capital towns: (i) Taxila: name of capital as well as kingdom, intensely populated and known for the fertility of its soil, (ii) Abisares (part of the tract lying between Jhelum and Chenab), (iii) Kingdom of elder Porus (also between Jhelum and Chenab), (iv) Glansians having 37 cities, (v) Gandharis (between Chenab and Ravi), (vi) Adraistai with its capital Pimprama (on the eastern side of Ravi), (vii) Cathaians (Gurdaspur and Amritsar districts) with capital Sangala (Fatehgarh in Gurdaspur district or Jandiala near Amritsar), (viii) Sophytes (Saubhuti, east of Jhelum), (ix) Phegelas (between Ravi and Beas), (x) Siboi (Shibi with its capital Shivapura,(both in Jhang district),(xi) Agalassoi (in the neighbourhood of Siboi), (xii) Oxydracae or Sudracao (Kshudraka, between Ravi and Beas), (xiii) Malloi (Malavs; between Chenab and Ravi), (xiv) Abastanai or Sambastai (Ambashtha, lower valley of Chenab), (xv-xvi) Xathroi and Ossadioi (Kshatri and Vasati; between the confluence of Chenab and Ravi and Chenab and Indus respectively).

Alexander founded a few cities in the Panjab bearing his name. Bucephala Alexandria was built on the west bank of Jhelum where his favourite charger Bucephalus died, Nicaia on the east bank of that river where Porus was defeated and the third Alexandria at the confluence of Chenab and Indus above the land of Sodrai and Massanoi of northern Sindh.

The *Periplus of the Erythraean Sea,* a book of information on commerce and navigation, composed about the middle or second half of the first century A.D., refers to certain places of the Panjab such as Aratrioi (Arattas), Gandaraooi (Gandhara), Proclais (Pushkalavati) and Bucephalus Alexandria. Of considerable value from our point is, of course, Ptolemy's *Treatise on Geography,* written about the middle of the second century A.D. Ptolemy supplies a long list of place-names and indicates their location by referring to the degrees of latitude and longitude which however are inaccurate, possibly because of his distorted view of the shape of India. He mentions Indus and its five tributaries – Bidaspes (Jhelum), Sandabal (Chenab), Adris or Rouadis (Iravati or Ravi), Bibasis (Vipasha or Beas) and Zarados (Shatadru or Sutlej) and also their confluences. He is aware of the peoples and territories of the Panjab. He mentions Gandarai, Arsa (tirasa-Hazara district), Pandoouoi (Paurava kingdom around Jhelum) and the cities Proclais (Pushkalavati), Naulibi, Ithagouros, Taxila, Labaka and Sagala (Sialkot; also called Euthedemia after its Greek conqueror Euthydemus of the early second century B.C.). Some of the cities could not be identified. Pandoouoi or the Paurava kingdom covered a wider area watered by the three rivers of the Panjab, namely, Jhelum, Chenab and Ravi, i.e., northern Sindh and parts of western Panjab up to the Sialkot region.

The Chinese Impressions

The next group of travellers visiting this part of India were Chinese; their main purpose being the study of Buddhism. Of these the most noteworthy are Fa-hien and Yuan Chwang. Fa-hien travelled in India in the early fifth century A.D. He came across a number of places in the Panjab in the course of his journey to eastern India. In his brief account he mentions Gandhara, Takshashila, Purushapura (Peshawar), He-lo (Hidda; west of Peshawar), Poh-na (Bannu) and Pe-too (Panchanada). More details are known from the account of Yuan Chwang, 'the king of travellers' who visited India in the first part of the 7th century A.D.[26] Gifted with a real aptitude for investigation Yuan Chwang may be classed among the most learned and illustrious geographers of the ancient world. Yuan Chwang provides exhaustive details of the places he visited in the Panjab: Gandhdara and Purushapura (the capital) were subject to Kapisha, Wo-to-ka-han-tu (Udabhanda; modern Und), Sha-lo-tu-lo (Shalatura; the birth place of Panini), Takshashila – then a dependency of Kashmir, had fertile soil yielding good crops with flowing streams, luxuriant vegetation and a genial climate; Seng-ha-pu-lo (Simhapura, a town on the eastern bank of the Indus), Wu-la-Shih (Urasa, modern Hazara), Pan-nu-Tsos (Punch) and Ho-lo-she-pu-lo (Rajapura; Rajauri), the last four being the dependencies of Kashmir. The account of the kingdom of Kashmir is fairly good. Yuan Chwang's next destinations were Cheh-ka (Takka), Sakala (Sialkot) to the east of which lay Chi-na-puh-ti (Chinabhukti) so called because of the association of a Chinese prince who was kept there as hostage by Kanishka, the Kushana emperor. Its (Chinabhukti) climate was warm, had abundant revenue, produced good crops but did not abound in trees. The traveller then mentions Tamasavana, She-lan-ta-lo (Jalandhar), Ku-lu-to (Kullu), She-to-tu-lu (region of the Sutlej valley; according to Cunningham it represented modern Sirhind), Sa-ta-ni-ssu-fa-lo (Thanesar) and Srughna (Sugh).

Observations of Muslim Geographers

Among the Persian sources *Hudud-al-Alam* (a work written in A.D. 982-83) and *Kitab-ul-Hind* of Al-Beruni (completed about A.D.1030) deserve particular mention. The *Hudud-al-Alam*[27] throws interesting light on conditions of some of the places of Panjab in respect of their merchandise, markets, coinage, towns and districts and nature of their government. It refers to Jalandhar as situated on a mountain in cold zone, Slapur (Simhapura), an important trade centre, Al-Jurz (perhaps Gujrat in Panjab; north of Chenab and south of Naoshera), Ohind (Vayhind) on the Indus, the capital of the Shahis,

Kashmir, Multan and Lahore. He describes most of these places as dependencies of the king of Kanauj which seems to be quite unlikely, for Kanauj was not then in a position to control such far off principalities.

The Kitab-ul-Hind shows thorough acquaintance with the rivers of Panjab-Indus and its five tributaries and the Sarasvati. It provides interesting details about their courses, the cities they pass through, and their union (excluding the Sarasvati) at a place called Panchanada below Multan. Its description of the routes passing through the Panjab as also the cities they joined is very useful. Among the cities relevant to the present study, Al-Biruni mentions Thanesar, Multan, Bamhanwa alias Al-Mansura, Sirsa, Pinjaur, Dahamala (the capital of Jalandhar), Ballawar (Vallapur, east of Jammu), Ladda, Rajagiri (Rajauri), Panipat, Kaithal, Sunnam, Adittahaur, Jajjanir, Mandahukur, the capital of Lahore, Waihind (Und), the capital of Kandhar (Gandhara), Purushawar (Peshawar), Babrahan (half way between Sindh and Jhelum, the best entrance from Panjab to Kashmir), Addishtan (Adhisthana or Shrinagar the capital of Kashmir) and Baramula. In his geographical knowledge Al-Biruni displays thorough understanding of Indian sources, the epics, the Puranas and works of well-known Indian astrologers.

We have thus presented a historical survey of the literature on the ancient geography of Panjab, its various territorial designations and the people who have largely contributed to the making of its composite culture.

Notes

1. *The New Encyclopaedia Britanica*, Vol.XV, 1980, p.285.
2. *Rigveda*, VII, 36.6.
3. *The Vedic Age* (ed.) R.C. Majumdar and A.D. Pusalkar, Bombay, 1951, pp. 241-44 (Geographical data), 215-50 (the tribes).
4. *History of the Punjab* (ed.) L.M. Joshi, Patiala, 1977, Vol.I, pp.31, 32.

5. G.P. Malalasekera, *Dictionary of Pali Proper Names*, Vol.I, London 1960, p.363.
6. *Anguttaranikaya*, Vol.I, (Nalanda ed.), p.197.
7. *Majjhimanikaya*, Vol.III, (Nalanda ed.) pp.131 ff; *Dighanikaya*, Vol.I, (Nalanda ed.) p.185; *Jataka*, Pt. I, Nalanda (ed.), pp.58, 156, 220.
8. *Mulasarvastivada-Vinaya*, Pt.I (ed.) S. Bagchi, Darbhanga, 1967, pp.8, 145,173, 184-90.
9. *Mahavastu* (Calcutta ed.) II, p. 564; *Majjhima*, I p.76; *Digha* (Nalanda ed.), II, p.217; *Majjhima*, II, p.281; Kurudhamma Jataka.
10. For details see P.C. Bagehi, *Sino-Indian Studies*, III, Parts 1-2, Calcutta, 1947.
11. Malalasekera, op.cit., III, pp.432-33, 1137, 1153-54, 1312; *Jataka*, (Nalanda ed.) Part I, pp.58, 233; Part II, p.246; *Majjhima*, II, p.405.
12. *Dipavamsa* (B.C. Law ed.), VIII, 4; *Mahavamsa*, N.K. Bhagwat (ed.), XII, 3,9.
13. Thomas Watters, *On Yuan Chwang's Travels in India*, I, p.265, reprint, Delhi 1961.
14. Thomas Watters, op.cit., I, pp.111-12, 261, 269, II, pp.88 ff, 91 ff; Samuel Beal, *Buddhist Records of the Western World*, reprint, Calcutta, 1958, pp.146-160, 162, 170, 180 etc.
    Rajatarangini (ed.) M.A. Stein, II, 101-07.
15. V.S. Agrawala, *Panini Kalina Bharata Varsha*, Varanasi, 1955, pp.49ff, 61 ff, 83 ff.
16. B.N. Puri, *India in the times of Patanjali*, Bombay, 1957, pp.70-72 (Physical Geography), 73-80 (Janapadas of North-West).
17. M. Winternitz, *Geschichte der Indischen Literatur*, Vol. I, English Tr. Mrs. S. Ketkar, Reprint, Delhi, 1972, pp.475, 576.
18. *Ramayana*, (Gorakhapur ed.), 1963, I, 6.22; 13.27; 55. 2-3; II. 8. 13-21; 70. 19-24; 71. 1-6; IV.43 11-12; VII. 101. 10-11; N.C. Das, *Ancient Geography of Asia Compiled from Valmiki Ramayana*, reprint, Varanasi, 1971, pp.29-35.
19. *History of the Punjab*, Vol. I, op.cit., p.170 (D.K. Gupta, "Punjab as Reflected in the Epics".
20. *Mahabharata* (Gorakhpur ed., 1956-58), Karnaparva (Chs. 40, 44-45), Shalyaparva (7-45), Sabhaparva (32.11) and Vanaparva (134.12) for description of Panchanada, Madra and Vahika.
21. *History of the Punjab*, op. cit., p.176.
22. For details of various kingdoms and peoples of Punjab see, *Adiparva*, 185, 6-23 (Draupadi-svayamvara), *Sabhaparva*, Chs 27, 32 (Arjuna and Nakula digvijaya) 34; *Vanaparva*, Chs 14-2; (Krishna's fight with the Salvas), Ch, 254(Karna-digvijaya) and *Udyogaparva* (for participants from Punjab in the great battle).

23. For geographical data in the Puranas see *Vayu*, 1.45, 109-39, *Matsya*, 113. 34-56; *Brahma*, Chs 18-20, 27; *Brahmanda*, 2. 6-40-68, *Padma*, Adi. Chs. 3-9; *Naradiya*, Purva Khanda Ch.3; *Markandeya*, Kurmavibhaga, Ch. 55 Bombay (ed.); *Garuda*, Purvardha, Ch.55; *Skanda*, Kumarika Khanda, Ch.69; *Brhannaradiya*, Purva Khanda, Ch. 56. 739-45; *Vamana*, 13.44, 53,59.
24. D.C. Sircar, op.cit., (*History of the Punjab*, p.39).
25. *The Classical Accounts of India*, ed. R.C. Majumdar, Calcutta, 1960, for 'Geography' Intro, pp. XV-XVII; Arrian, *Anabasis of Alexander*, p.5 ff, *Periplus Maris Erythraei*, p.288 ff, Pliny, *Naturalis Historia* (*The Natural History*), p.337 ff, Plotemy, *Treatise on Geography*, p.351 ff.
26. *The Travels of Fa-hien* ed. James Legges, reprint, Delhi, 1971, pp.31-42; Thomas Watters, *On Yuan Chwang's Travels in India*, Reprint, Delhi, 1961. pp.198-300, 315-2.
27. *Hudud-al-Alam* (The Regions of the World), translated and explained by V. Minorsky, E.J.W. Gibb Memorial Series, Vol. XI, Oxford, 1937; *Al-Beruni's India*, ed. E.C. Sachu; Reprint, Delhi, 1964, pp.205-08, (Part I, Ch.XVIII, 'Geography').

Select Bibliography

Cunningham, A., *The Ancient Geography of India*, Reprint, Varanasi, 1963.

Dey, N.L., *Geographical Dictionary of Ancient and Medieval India*, Reprint, New Delhi, 1971.

Law, B.C., *Historical Geography of Ancient India*, Paris, 1954; *India as described in Early Texts of Jainism and Buddhism*, London, 1941.

Raychaudhuri, H.C., *Studies in Indian Antiquities* (Puranic Geography and Cosmography), Calcutta, 1959.

Sircar, D.C., *Studies in the Geography of Ancient and Medieval India*, Delhi, 1960; *Ancient Geography of the Punjab*, in *History of the Punjab* ed. L.M. Joshi, Vol. I, Patiala, 1947, p.25 ff.

Upadhyaya, Bharat Singh, *Buddhakalina Bharatiya Bhugola*, Allahabad, 1961.

Vidyalankar, Jayachandra, *Bharata Bhumi Aur Usake Nivasi*, 1930.

7

Trends in the Historiography of Panjab

Historical studies in India during the present century reveal three distinctive trends, namely, the imperial, the nationalist and the scientific, the last providing a critical analytical study of the sources primarily based on socio economic formations. As rightly pointed out by Romila Thapar, "The initial interest in India in regional history grew out of nationalist historical writings. It was motivated to some extent by a search for new source-material .... It is, however, at the interpretational level that the interest in regional history assumes greater historiographic potential, a potential with which we are perhaps not altogether fully familiar." The regional studies do not form any special category and may quite reasonably be included under the last two categories of historical writings mentioned above. It is perhaps instinctive in human beings to develop emotional attachment to the place of their association, an attachment which they carry till the last moments of their life. However, a scientific study of this aspect of the human existence can only be possible through an understanding of its socio-economic foundation so brilliantly put by F. Engels in his thesis, "The Origin of the Family, Private Property and the State".

The Panjab which came in the scheme of the British imperial expansion much later, did not have the early advantage of the introduction of the English system of education as Calcutta, Madras or Bombay Presidencies had, and it could not be in a position to be proud of any work particularly on the reconstruction of the earliest phases of its historical growth which may stand in comparison to R.G. Bandarkar's *Early History of the Deccan*, K.S. Aiyangar's *Contributions to South Indian History and Culture* or R.C. Majumdar edited, *The History of Bengal* (particularly in those portions where regional/nationalist tendency is not so pronounced). Syad Muhammad Latif's *History of the Panjab* carries one section on the ancient period but it is based on secondary sources of the British historians and has no pretension for any originality. Sita Ram Kohali's monograph on the "Indus Valley Civilisation" is similarly devoid of information based on first-hand study of either literary or archaeological sources. Haryana, on the other hand, has a different story to tell. In the sense of a geographical entity it was not known before 12th century. As an administrative unit its fortunes were tied either with Delhi, Northwestern Province or Panjab. And further perhaps for its role in the uprising of 1857 and the subsequent activities of the Wahabis, it had to suffer and struggle for long, to find its historical identity. In view of this, historical consciousness came to the region very late. The earlier writings on aspects of its history are therefore, concerned more with compilation of the original source-material rather than providing any systematic historical reconstruction of the region. It is only recently that the scholars of the Kurukshetra University have taken up the task of providing comprehensive account of the history, archaeology and culture of the new state. The importance of such painstaking research cannot be gainsaid but this has to be pursued not in isolation but in an objective spirit, in relevance to the general historical growth of the country.

In the case of the Panjab (a term being used here in its wider connotation i.e., former United Panjab) one is surprised to find that no comprehensive work on its ancient period has so far been written. The *History of the Punjab* (2 Vols.), prepared under the able guidance of the late Fauja Singh and his distinguished colleague the late L.M. Joshi, is perhaps the first such attempt in this direction. But being a collective venture it has its disadvantages such as lack of literary unity, uniformity of organisation and planning which we do not find in works produced by single controlling mind. The chapter on pre-history and proto-history for instance, is just a survey, negligible as far as the interpretative part is concerned, and consequently does not help historical reconstruction. The chapter on Buddhism is sketchy although much material is available on the subject while there is no chapter on Jainism although it did not disappear like Buddhism from the region and the business community which substantially supported it in the days of yore, still has its share in sustaining the economy of the state even today. However, despite these shortcomings, as rightly pointed out by the editors, the importance of the work is unquestionable. It has indeed paved the way for further intensive research on the historical growth of the Panjab.

The absence of comprehensive history of the ancient Panjab may perhaps be explained as due to the extensive coverage given to this region in the general histories on ancient India specially because it was in this land of the five rivers (Panchanada) or seven rivers (Saptasindhu), the foundations of the earliest cultures of India were laid. One of the earliest homosapians roamed about in its valleys and then after a long pause, civic and social life began to develop gradually at its various pre-historic and proto-historic sites, and it was again here quite recently that the clear breach between the Harappans and the Aryans was bridged for the first time at Bhagwanpura. It has always been the land of plenty, the very heaven on earth as known to the Indian tradition and finally it was in this region that many decisive actions of Indian history took place and where powers of oppression were defied even in face of great adversity. But soon after India gained independence and various states were reorganised, an urgent need must have been felt to find identities in the states where these were absent and attempts at re-writing the history of these regions were initiated.

In V.A. Smith's *The Early History of India*, considerable space (about 66 of the 478 pages) is devoted for the first time in dealing with Alexander's campaign in the Panjab and is based on the classical accounts as well as on the results of the labour of modern geographers and early archaeologists. The work which is a classical example of the imperialistic approach to the study of ancient India, also provides in a lucid style a consecutive and systematic account of a phase of the history of Panjab at the time of Alexander's invasion (as becomes explicit from its sub-title). His detailed treatment of Alexander's Indian campaign may be explained besides his basic approach as also due to the availability of source-material to which he must have an easy excess. The value of Smith's work on this part of Indian history cannot be minimised also taking into account his contribution to the history of the Indo-Greeks, the Indo-Parthians and the Indo-Scythians who ruled over considerable portion of the Panjab during the post-Mauryan period.

During the nineteenth and the early decades of the present century historical studies in India were pressed into service as the handmaid of politics, in favour of religious, social and later, political reforms and hence the glories of the past were more emphasised to encourage the rising national spirit of India. This nationalist-revivalist trend in Indian historiography is best represented in the works of K.P. Jayaswal particularly *Hindu Polity* and the *History of India*, the first was dedicated quite significantly to the memory of Republicans including the Kathas of the Panjab who announced, the "Philosophies of Freedom". R.K. Mookerji's *Fundamental Unity of India* although more restrained, was likewise written to serve a political purpose. Several lesser historians also employed their talents for similar ends and traces of this kind of propaganda can be found in many works of this period. The nationalistic bias in the historical writings becomes more explicit in the debate over the original home of the Aryans where Indologists like A.C. Das, Sampurnanand and Ganganath Jha strongly defend the claim of the land of the seven rivers on the basis of their interpretation of the literary tradition. But quite different was the approach of K.M. Panikkar, Subba Rao and H.C. Raychaudhuri whose study of the influence of geographical factors on historical growth of various regions of India was based on scientific footing, the last named scholar in his *Studies in Indian Antiquities* deals with geography, while his articles on "The Vedic Sarasvati" and the "Antiquity of the Rigveda" have special relevance to the Panjab. In general, Raychaudhuri is cautious and restrained and does not show any tangible nationalistic influence and succeeds in keeping his times out of his work, in a period when tendency toward regional nationalism was quite noticeable in historical writings. His *Political History of Ancient India* which covers also Panjab stands remarkable for its critical approach, originality of conception and breadth of vision. Basham has rightly called it the work of a 'first class mind'. The task of Raychaudhuri was carried further by his distinguished pupil, D.C. Sircar by contributing substantially to the historical geography of the Panjab.

So far we have taken into consideration those writings which are general histories of India but which also take sufficient note of the developments in the Panjab. These writings can be classified under imperialistic or nationalistic or in some cases on the lines founded by Ranke.

Among historians who have made substantial contributions to the history and culture of the Panjab including Haryana, Buddha Prakash who presided over the Ancient Section of the First Panjab History Conference (in 1965), deserves special mention. His contributions to the regional history are: *Political and Social Movements in Ancient Panjab* (Delhi, 1963), *Glimpses of Ancient Panjab* (Sita Ram Kohli Memorial Lectures, Patiala, 1966), *Rigveda and the Indus Civilisation* (Hoshiarpur, 1966), *Hariyana Through the Ages*

(Kurukshetra, 1967), *Evolution of Heroic Tradition in Ancient Panjab* (Patiala, 1971) and several other research papers. His *Rigveda and the Indus Civilisation* is an attempt to correlate the relics found at Mohenjodaro and Harappa with the literary evidence of the *Rigveda* in justification of the view that the authors of the Indus civilisation were, in fact, Aryans and not Dravidians; *The Political and Social Movement in Ancient Panjab* was severely criticised by R.C. Majumdar (*Journal of Indian History,* 1964) for the philological basis of the author's historical inferences while there are others who considered it 'thought provoking'; *Hariyana Through the Ages* is just a survey and provides very little for a serious researcher by way of new interpretation or detailed analysis of the source-material available. The *Evolution of Heroic Tradition in Ancient Panjab* was written at a time when Indo-Pakistan relations had become extremely tense due to developments in East Pakistan and the need to keep burning patriotic feelings of the people against any serious threat to the national security was intensely felt. It is very difficult to say to which ideology he belonged. In his addresses he speaks of Gandhi and non-alignment, he also quotes from the writings of Marx and Toynbee, the latter's writings were subject of his special interest and study so much so that one of his reviewers even went to the extent of calling him 'Indian Toynbee'. A careful survey of Buddha Prakash's writings does not disclose any definite ideology to which he belonged nor his observations on India's historical growth seem to be based on solid scientific foundation which could only be laid by a critical and analytical study of all types of source-material available. This is particularly baffling to some of us who have the opportunity of coming in his close contact; all the more when they find that he had been a serious student of historiography and had also taught this branch of study for considerable period of time. I had occasion to visit his library at Saharanpur, full of rare manuscripts and books and also talking to the members of his family who were desirous of setting a research institution in his memory. Buddha Prakash was a voracious reader and was conversant with a number of languages. Perhaps, his philological and linguistic preference prevented him from proceeding on scientific lines and as viewed by the psychologists, writings of individuals which, of course, include the historian, are better judged by an understanding of the conditions that shape and influence their 'thought process' and herein perhaps lies the answer to some of the questions which occur in the mind while going through what he wrote. It cannot be denied that the geographical factors tremendously influence historical process and in a big way it is true of this region where decisive battles of Indian history were fought. To fight for one's existence, for the values one stands for, or for the defence of the land threatened by foreign invasions is instinctive and inborn in human beings and can be explained rationally. This may be true of any people under similar circumstances. The forces of nature by themselves are dead perhaps appropriately explained by the term *jada* of the Indian philosophical tradition. These forces become alive when they come in contact with human beings. History, in fact, begins with the advent of man with his acceptance of the challenge of nature and exploiting it for better conditions of life. This process makes the nature alive (*chetana*) and gives it a meaning. Religious and cultural significance of a region does not depend necessarily as Buddha Prakash maintains on geo-political factors alone but basically on the consciousness of man of his conditions specially his socio-economic necessities which induce his mental capacity to device means to simplify the natural forces for a better and happy life. Religion and culture need to be properly understood in this perspective. One wonders if the professor believed like Toynbee in the vital role of supernatural forces in the historical process, for at times one sees a mystical touch in his writings or does he, in fact, impose a thesis on facts or was he inspired by Toynbee's contention that great moments in history were not those when empires were built or inventions took place, but when great religions were born? To understand Buddha Prakash one has to go through his approach to Toynbee's *Study of History*.

Towards the middle of the present century the influence of Marxism started reflecting in the writings of some younger historians of ancient India more remarkably in the works of D.D. Kosambi who is universally acknowledged as the founder of that school in India. Nevertheless one is really puzzled at the satisfaction of such eminent historian as A.L. Basham that Marxism "does not appear to have affected any of the authorities (he had) mentioned". Basham advices "that the historians of Ancient India should continue to work with a minimum of 'fundamental presupposition' in an attempt to discover with some degree of certainty 'what happened' for the history of Ancient India is at present too tenacious that it can be fitted into almost any preconceived pattern". It may be of interest to note that Basham's comments were made in 1961 while Kosambi's *Introduction to the Study of Indian History* appeared in 1956 about five years earlier and he did not even care to take notice of the latter's approach to Indian history particularly when one sees how profoundly it has influenced the succeeding generation of scholars judging by the type of questions being raised and answers given in historical conferences and congresses in recent times. Besides the *Introduction*, D.D. Kosambi's other work is *The Culture and Civilization of Ancient India in Historical Outline* (London, 1965) both written in very effective style, strike at the very root of traditional approach to the study of Indian history. The importance of the latter work can be well understood from the remark of the author who asks us to regard his other works as 'footnotes' to this one. Although his works in general attempt at a historical reconstruction of India on a scientific basis they do cover the region with which we are concerned here and hence their brief evaluation. Unlike Dange and others, Kosambi does not think that Indian history precisely fits into Marxist scheme of periodisation. While elaborating, he points out that ancient Indian society unlike the Greek and the Roman, cannot be characterised as based on slavery. Challenging 'the unchangeableness of Asiatic Societies' as conceived by Marx and Engels, he suggests that "the very formation of the village economy with the plough used on a fixed plot of land implies a tremendous advance in the means of production". History for Kosambi is displayed in full detail in the villages of India, provided one has the vision and insight to read that history. The succession of seasons he connects with the traditional concept of 'four yugas' reflecting four major changes of season accurately, which in a big way effect the village economy. Similarly, his study of the customs, beliefs and traditions of the village folks to show how very ancient observances can survive with little change of outward form to this day, is indeed thought provoking. The questions of his deep concern are: Did the change from food gathering and the pastoral life to agriculture make new religion necessary? Who were the Aryans? If any. Did the caste system ever serve any useful purpose? For any investigation into the earliest phases of the history of Panjab whose economy is still basically an agricultural economy, answers to the questions which Kosambi has so brilliantly posed, would be very rewarding.

As pointed out by D.N. Jha, for Kosambi Marxism is not a 'substitute of thinking' but a 'tool of analysis' the importance of which was realised even by Gorden Childe much before. The adoption of Marx's thesis according to him does not imply blind repetition of all his conclusions (and even less those of the official party-line Marxists) at all times. He remains a Marxist in so far as he maintains that "history is the presentation in chronological order of successive changes in the means and relations of production". For him, the main question is not who was the king but whether the people used plough: light or heavy. Dynastic changes, however, may be studied in so far as they indicate "powerful changes in the productive basis". Accordingly, Kosambi treats culture as the "essential ways of the life of the whole people" and does not regard it purely as "a matter of intellectual and spiritual values". He is very much aware of the nature of the source material and the difficulty which it puts in the way of historical reconstruction he desires to make. During the period, when he wrote, even archaeology was not advanced enough to solve the really important questions not even to ask some of them. Therefore, in his methodology he followed the technique of collation of written records with archaeology and the interpretation of each of these in conjunction with ethnography ("Combined Methodology in Indology", *Indo Iranian Journal,* Vol. VI.).

The capital fact of Indian history according to him is the continuous process of fusion of tribal elements into the general society and hence the process of mutual acculturation between the food-producing advanced immigrants and the food-gathering aboriginals. This needs to be underlined.

Introducing the reader to the pre-historic civilisation of the Indus Valley, Kosambi explains why the first great urban development on the sub-continent should have taken place along the river that flows across a virtual desert. The river is necessary for water and fish, an important source of food, the alluvial desert keeps the early population confined to a strip along the river making food gathering beyond a certain stage and range impossible and giving stimulus to the development of a food-producing economy with the surplus necessary for maintenance of urban centres. The Indus settlements were sparse, there were only two large cities which he attributes to the absence of canal irrigation and heavy plough. Much evidence has come to light since Kosambi wrote and his views need to be revised in the light of the latest position. His other observations connecting the 'Great Bath' at Mohenjodaro with a ritual tank originally connected with primitive fertility rites, a prototype of the later sacred pond (Pushkara) and that "the internal economic distribution was administered by the great temple and its priesthood" need thorough examination. Similarly may be treated his other suggestion that Harappan state was theocratic and that the Aryans brought about the ruins of Indus cities, the last is partially true and needs to be reviewed in the light of the latest archaeological evidence which suggest a variety of factors which led towards that end.

The definite technological superiority of the new people – the Aryans, over their predecessors was because of their mastery of the use of plough and iron. They were pastoral, nomadic, patriarchal and used horse-chariots. The origin of Indian caste-system, Kosambi traces to the fusion of the Aryans with the non-Aryan elements specially the Brahmana caste, a fundamentally new proposition which may be most unwelcome and shocking to that group of historians who are staunch supporters of an "Indian home for the Aryans and an unequalled purity for their blood". Although believing that ideas do effect social development one is surprised to see why Kosambi did not take into account the effects of natural causes or superstitious beliefs in the proliferation of the Indian caste system, as rightly pointed out by D.N. Jha.

The ideological basis of the feudal society Kosambi attempts to find in the doctrine of the *Bhakti* as propounded in the Gita. This proposition cannot be accepted on chronological grounds alone. Bhakti or the relationship between the god and his devotee cannot be equated with the personal relationship as it subsisted in feudal times. Similarly, his assertation that the Gita with its "brilliant Sanskrit and superb inconsistency is a book that allows the reader to justify almost any action while shrugging of the consequence" is uncalled for, missing completely the true spirit of the Gita.

One may generally disagree with the views of Kosambi on the Gita but one cannot but appreciate the boldness with which they were formulated and which are not without some relevance even today. Investigation into various strata of the philosophical and ethical contents of the Gita to find out which of these are the oldest and represent, if at all, the period when the conflict between the Bharata tribes took place, may be considered as reasonable academic activity, but one is really disturbed and feels very much concerned when Sanskrit scholars without any background of history come forward with statements on the identification of the place where the Gita was proclaimed and mislead the people by giving false notions about their history and culture. The matter becomes worst when men in the highest authority make promises of rewards for any such misconceived adventure and make mockery of our whole academic existence.

Among the historians who furthered the line so well drawn by D.D. Kosambi, R.S. Sharma deserves special mention. Well known for his studies on the socio-economic history of ancient India particularly *Indian Feudalism* and the *Position of the Shudras,* the latest being *Material Culture and Social Formation in Ancient India* which has relevance to the ancient history of the Panjab. The last work brings out in an integrated manner the evolution of material and social formations of the Indo-Gangetic plains during the Vedic and post-Vedic times classified quite reasonably by the author in three stages namely, the tribal, the proto-class, proto-state and that based on class and state.

Sharma bases his study mainly on literary sources for the early-Vedic period because of the inavailability of archaeological evidence. He makes indepth study of such problems as the pastoral nature of economy without any surplus, the tribal conflicts which made war 'a natural economic function' and the unequal sharing of wealth which led to the emergence of the institution of a Raja. His study of such Vedic terms as *Grama, Gotra, Jana* or *Visha* to explain the nature of pastoral economy is enlightening. The distinction between the upper *varnas* and the commoners he rightly explains as due to the system of division of labour and ritual status. The Painted Grey Ware culture, characterised by the introduction of iron technology, expansion of plough agriculture and the growth of permanent rural settlements, marks the transition from the early Vedic to the later-Vedic age which consequently led to the shifting of the activities of the people to the Indo-Gangetic divide and western Gangetic plains. The limited surplus available in these changing circumstances had therefore a limited role in respect of the economic function of the state. The author explains the existence of the joint ownerships of the land due to undeveloped or primitive technology. The burden of the tax mainly fell on the peasant while the beneficiaries were the priests and Kshatriyas who did not participate in the productive process. The internal contradiction of the varnas he attributes and rightly so, to the unequal system of distribution. During the period of the Mahajanapadas (i.e., the proto-state period), polity was dominated by chiefs and princes, no regular system of taxation emerged and that tribal militia was replaced by peasant militia for which he adduces evidence from the texts. The ritualistic nature of the religion Sharma explains as the need of the time for making the peasants obey and pay taxes to the chief a tendency which reflects the growing alienation of the peasants in the new social formation. The impact of Kosambi on Sharma is clearly discernable in his study of the process of assimilation of Vedic and non-Vedic people which led to the emergence of the priestly class. But it may be difficult to agree with Sharma's assumption that the expansion of settlements started from the 'Age of the Buddha' through forest clearance, a phenomenon which can be traced to an early period as reflected in the Gautama-Rahugana and Videgha Mathava narratives referring to the carrying of the sacred fire from the banks of the Sarasvati to the banks of Sadanira or the burning of the Khandava of the epic tradition which may represent happenings of much earlier period. One has to follow the approach of D.D. Kosambi in analysing such 'myths' to find the 'reality'. It is true that centre of gravity was shifted to the eastern regions in the 'Age of the Buddha' which is archaeologically called the Northern Black Polished Ware (NBP) phase but one would like to know why Buddha frequently visited the Kurus and why there are repeated references to their moral and ethical code of conduct in the early Buddhist literature? The *varna* system was devised according to him for legal and ideological justification of obedience to the king and the priests by way of paying taxes and gifts to them. The higher status of the upper-classes was upheld on the concept of purity based on contempt for manual labour resulting in effect in the exploitation of the producing classes. One is tempted to repeat what D.N. Jha has observed in his study of Sharma's illustrious predecessor Kosambi regarding the role of the natural factors and superstitious beliefs in the proliferation of the Indian caste system. It would be of interest to know how did these factors namely, changing of the rivers courses, drying up of their waters, droughts, famines, floods, and earthquakes have effected the socio-economic formations. The terror of the destructive power of nature must have also led to the formations of superstitious beliefs of these early people. The various Vedic and Puranic legends wherein such elements are reflected in a different garb also need scientific investigation.

The opposition of Buddhism to animal sacrifices, permission to moneylending, slavery and urban mode of life and their effects on change in the mode of production and the recommendation of charity to soften the rigours of the unjust *varna* system have been very convincingly explained by Sharma. However, it may be pointed out that some of these were already there in the post-Vedic if not in the later-Vedic periods, and can also be found in the Upanishadic spirit of revolt against ritualism and in their advocacy of the concept of charity. May it be pointed out that some of the Upanishadas are pre-Buddha, a fact which can be established on the basis of the same stratigraphical and comparative method used by Sharma?

Sharma does not agree with some archaeologists using the term 'Iron Age' for the later-Vedic Painted Grey Ware (PGW) period. The character of iron technology was negligible in agriculture and low level of industrial production which according to Sharma, was the major constraint in the growth of urbanisation and emergence of state in later-Vedic formation. But there was an urbanisation even without the knowledge of iron before. Why? As rightly pointed out by Suraj Bhan "it can best be called a copper-iron-age to distinguish this transitional stage from the preceding post-Harappan Copper Age and the succeeding NBP period which is full-fledged 'Iron Age' ".

Sharma's identification of the Rigvedic peoples with pre-Iron-post-Harappan peasant communities would indeed be inspiring to the archaeologist for applying similar method for detecting the material relics of the pastoral Rigvedic tribes and understanding the material in the light of the nature of the social formation indicated by comparison. As rightly pointed out by Suraj Bhan, this approach would help in exposing the fallacies of certain archaeologists and Indologists in their identification of the Rigvedic pastoral tribal people disclosing lack of historical perspective and a subjective approach even in archaeology.

The change from one social formation to another, Sharma explains by following historical materialistic method based on an in-depth study of the fundamental propositions of Marx, Engels, Morgan, Gordan Childe and others in the fields of archaeology, anthropology and also sociology although very much aware he is of the inadequacies of the last two disciplines. For Sharma social history does not mean "a backward projection of sociology" nor is economic history "an appreciation of economic theory with retrospective effects".

His method based on critical comparative and scientific study of the various sources helps admirably in providing a clear understanding of the process of social evolution in ancient India. This includes stratigraphical study of the texts, comparative linguistics and application even of statistics and ethnography which have been similarly used by Kosambi in his writings before. The work for its sound and lucid analysis of the social formation has been rightly hailed as of "outstanding value, indispensable for all serious students of Ancient Indian history and archaeology".

In his studies on 'feudalism', Sharma points out that the Agrahara land-grants with which is traced the origin and development of feudalism, is absent in the Panjab. This practice is generally linked with decline of trade and commerce and consequently of towns and lesser use of money. This too does not seem to be the case with Panjab as is gathered from the

Chinese and Arab accounts confirmed also by contemporary literature. Sharma feels that probably the wider use of silver and copper coins obviated the need for payment through the land-grants. In Haryana particularly transfer of royal income from trade and commerce to religious beneficiaries was prevalent.

Romila Thapar in her presidential address (Panjab History Conference, 1976) has discussed 'the scope and significance of regional history' in the context of the Panjab, the subject which she has rightly pointed out "merits attention not only of the specialist in the region but also of historians working on other aspects of Indian History". It was in the inter-imperial periods that the nature of historical change at the regional level is seen more clearly. Regional history thus becomes a corrective to the earlier tendency to generalise about the sub-continent from the perspective of the Ganga valley. The spread of nationalism into various states increased the interest in regional history in modern times. It can be seen in contemporary writings where attempts are made to equate the present day boundary of a region as viable for all periods of its history. Thapar explains how the conventional periodisation into 'ancient, medieval and modern' imposes assumption on the historical data from regional sources and points out that the evidence supports neither the assumption nor the time-brackets. She contends that the convenience in such periodisation should not be allowed to become an intellectual truth. The theory of Aryan origin of culture and social stratification deviates from the prescribed norm, a phenomenon which can be explained only by investigating the actual caste stratification at various historical times. Thapar further points out how search for a golden period is often identified "as the period to which the currently dominant group traces its roots and is described in the glowing tints of cultural resurgence. Golden age have to shift as new social groups come to the fore and they have the disadvantage that they focus on a particular series of historical events often to the near exclusion of others of equal importance".

The positive side of the regional history writing can be explained in terms of analysis of the historical pattern of the region and the relations of these patterns to the generalisation of Indian history. The testing of such generalisation would thus involve the understanding of the pattern of historical change at the regional level. The interaction and relationship between various sub-regions of Panjab have been of a complex character and have never been consistent and similar through time. One of its potent reasons being hydrographic disturbances, involving the Sarasvati, the Beas and the Ravi. The influence of ecological factors on cultural formations of the earlier periods of the history of the Panjab, Thapar precisely explains on the basis of archaeological evidence. The economic factors also contribute to the history of the region. The schemes of imperial expansion in the region, for instance, may in part have been motivated by the wish to control not only strategic entrance into the sub-continent but also the trade routes. Thapar may perhaps be right in her contention that the persistence of tribal republics in this region suggest relative autonomy from interference by strong political powers but it would be difficult to agree with the next part of her observation that such interference would have been inevitable had it been a rich, agricultural region which is not based on evidence. Further, it was certainly not the reason for Harshavardhana's shifting of his capital to the Ganga valley. The prosperity of the region is confirmed by foreign accounts as well as indigenous literary evidence. Similarly, the absence of the land-grants from Panjab need not necessarily show lesser importance of agriculture, her alternate suggestion that perhaps an agrarian and administrative system which did not require the kind of changes taking place in neighbouring region seem to be more plausible. This feature has already been taken note of in connection with Sharma's historical writings. The destruction of temples by the Turk invaders is gathered from the Muslim accounts and is further confirmed by archaeological explorations and it is not 'simply a conventional explanation' as Thapar would like us to believe. The observation on the declining role of Brahmanism in the latter part of the first millennium A.D. in the religion of the area and also on the pattern of caste formation and caste structure is very interesting. Further, it has been pointed out that in the hill states it had a firm foothold and the process of acculturation is more evident there. These suggestions are pertinent and need further elaboration by researchers in the field. The emergence of the Khatris, Thapar explains in the context of the Turkish invasions which opened trade routes to central Asia which were under the control of Mahmud of Ghazni and draws attention to the fact that Mahmud, in course of his march, had cities like Multan, Thanesar, Kanauj, Mathura and Somnath as his prize targets.

An analytical survey of the role of agriculture technology in historical change in the Panjab, Thapar carries to the succeeding periods, also taking into account the linkage between the popular religious sects and various castes, an aspect which is crucial not merely to the history of a religious movement but also to the social pattern of the region. The emergence of the kingdom of the Panjab as rightly pointed out, is not a sudden development of modern times but it has a long gestation period which needs to be studied in the light of the various trends to which Thapar draws out attention. It is here, in connecting these elements regional history can contribute substantially. "If the focus on the pattern of historical change in the region can be sharpened, it should contribute to the quality of generalisation at the broader level as well as make for more valuable comparative studies with other regions". The similarities in such studies enable a wider generalisation while dissimilarities would indicate the particular regional factors and would lead to the modification of the broader generalisation. For any serious researcher on the history of Panjab, this brilliant exposition of the scope and significance of regional history based on a comparative historical method of inquiry is commendable and needs serious consideration. And finally, the boldness of conception which is reflected in Thapar's concluding remark that "even a movement as powerful as that of Sikhism and the emergence of the kingdom of the Panjab can become a viable historical study only in the context of the totality of the history of the Panjab" and the "historical events are not isolated phenomenon suspended in space and time, and the historical matrix in which they are embedded is as important as the event" deserve our full appreciation.

Lallanji Gopal, in his various studies, while stressing the importance of archaeological sources for unravelling the mysteries of India's early history, takes note also of the role of the geographical factors. For the reconstruction of the post-Mauryan period of the Panjab, numismatic evidence is of exceptional value. The application of models in historical research and its limitations and the problem of social relevance in such writings draws Gopal's special attention. He recognises 'meaning and significance' of history for each generation and rightly rejects the idea of absolute history for objectivity in history is distinct from that obtained in sciences. According to him "the consciousness of the ideal and a sincere effort to achieve it within the limitations imposed by the 'object' are in themselves achievements of considerable significance'. Lessons of history he maintains "should be used to correct past mistakes" so as to "improve our present" and not to perpetuate the fallacies showing thereby his awareness of the radical changes in the historical situation. Discussing the use of history for political purposes by the imperialist, nationalist and some of the Marxist historians, he points out that difficulty begins when "for reasons of commitment to the political ideology, facts contrary to the formulation of the theory are deliberately suppressed and conflicting details are ironed out by forced and twisted interpretation". Nevertheless, Gopal has appreciation for the Marxist interpretation applied in 'an honest academic fashion', and which should not be used he warns, for non-academic purpose.

Feeling concerned about the problems involved in rigid approach towards the stages of evolution as suggested by Marx, Gopal is also aware of the usefulness of Marx's interpretation of the socio-economic factors involved in the historical process of growth which thus provide a wider canvas and a proper perspective to history. A liberal interpretation of Marxist theory Gopal considers vital for the study of the evolution of science and technology and for determining the various changes in the mode of production. This should in fact form the basis of a scientific reconstruction of the social and economic history, he maintains. Basically a master of economic history of ancient India Gopal surveys the different stages of the economic growth of the ancient Panjab, its trade relations with countries beyond western borders of India, marked by the resulting prosperity as indicated by the rise of towns and the progress of the urban economy. The role of the Buddhist missionary and that of the merchant community in the expansion of Indian culture were complementary.

Gopal attempts at investigating into the discovery of the present characteristics of the economic life of Panjab namely, agriculture, crafts, merchandise, organisation of trade and monopoly of the market in its earlier periods. The account of foreign travellers together with the archaeological evidence has been very fruitfully used while dealing with the problem of assimilation of the foreign elements in the social system of the Panjab, admitting of course, the limitations put by the paucity of relevant evidence in this type of research. The evidence of Al-Beruni and *Devalasmriti* shows that people forcibly abducted, converted and made captive, could regain their original status by following purification rites. This is of particular interest for researchers on social history of the Panjab and needs thorough investigation.

So far we have taken into account the approach followed and methods employed by historians in their writings which is relevant to the historiography of the Panjab. We shall lastly proceed to evaluate the writings of Suraj Bhan, the archaeologist, who has recently made a strong plea for historical approach in his address to the Panjab History Conference before and also to a section of the Indian History Congress Session held at Srinagar (1985). The theme which principally concerns Bhan is the genesis, growth and the decline of first urbanisation in ancient Panjab. For such reconstruction the best approach is historical and archaeology being the primary source has to be integrated for such a task.

Suraj Bhan explains the changing character of archaeology due to scientific techniques of stratification, exploration and excavation and an understanding of the role of environment in historical process of growth. As rightly pointed out by him, this new method of scientific classification and interpretation of archaeological evidence starts from V. Gordon Childe to reveal trends and patterns of social developments. One of the most important features of archaeological study according to Childe was emphasis on the use of typology. The archaeological evidence accordingly was used for the reconstruction of effective environment of past societies and later its comparison with other contemporary societies of the world have widened the scope of such investigation. Underlining the limitations of ethnography Childe made it clear that a study of social evolution could only be made possible by arranging types in logical series. Childe was the advocate of rational approach for understanding causation in history, and hence he did not see the past as past. This revolutionary trend which put archaeological investigation on sound scientific foundation, looked at culture as a system or totality of divergent facts interacting on one another. Suraj Bhan also draws attention to further new trends which were introduced by L. Binford and Mark Leone namely, cultural ecology, system theory, use of computerised statistics thus leading to inter-disciplinary approach to the study of cultural change based on data collection, chronology, cultural sequence and environmental reconstruction. The idea of 'New Archaeology' also comes under his fire for its claims for evolution of a scientific method of interpretation to explain cultural change without any satisfactory achievement to its credit. Admitting the contributions of the techniques of dating, collection and analysis of archaeological data to the understanding of technology, ecology, chronology and some of the cultural patterns, he maintains that the crucial factor is understanding the stages of socio-economic change and its role in determining the cultural formation and the process of their evolution. To explain his formulations Suraj Bhan proceeds with a brief survey of the earlier stages of socio-economic formations. viz., the Neolithic food-gathering stage, the growth of permanent settlements of farming communities knowing copper metallurgy and the use of wheel-made pottery and the early Chalcolithic cultures where agriculture had emerged and then turns to the main problem of the origin, growth and decline of Indus civilisation.

Rejecting Wheeler's idea of a rather sudden or an offspring of 'opportunity and genius' or Mesopotamian origin of the Indus civilisation or that of Fairservis of a "logical culmination of the cultural process already underway in the boarder lands of the sub-continent", Suraj Bhan quite convincingly attributes it to the socio-economic formation which served as the base for the cultural pattern of the Indus civilisation underlying its surplus generating economy and technological innovations. The origin and decline of this proto-historic urbanisation therefore, can be understood only after an integrating study of its socio-economic and cultural background. He rightly points out the decisive role of the changes in the forces of production in the promotion or retardation of changes in the socio-cultural formations. Suraj Bhan recognises the contributions of A. Ghosh in explaining the genesis of the Harappan culture by integrated study of the different pre-Harappan cultures of Indus-Ghaggar planes. According to Suraj Bhan the expansions of this culture was not due to any colonisation from outside, rather it was a consequence of the waking up of the people to the advantages of the new mode of life.

In his analytical study he points out that Harappan culture had no uniform or homogenous pattern in the region of Panjab. The rural culture, on the other hand, was more homogenous than the urban and that the elements of the elitist urban culture got mixed up with local culture of the masses. A. Ghosh has shown earlier that its population was not homogenous racially and its social formations showed composition of several classes. This complex nature of Harappan society is not properly studied in the absence of theoretical perspective or lack of adequate information from different categories of settlements particularly from village sites. Absence of stratigraphical digging led to speculations.

While discussing the causes of the decline of Harappan culture, Suraj Bhan takes note of the excavation of Y.D. Sharma at Ropar and Bara suggesting continuity of the culture in a transformed form, the regional pattern of post-Harappan culture (*c.* 1800-1300 B.C.) together with its coexistence with the Harappans, the views of Gordon Childe, Wheeler and Stuart Piggot making Rigvedic Aryans responsible for it and that of Raikes, Dales, S.R. Rao and A. Ghosh stressing the role of ecological, climatic and geomorphological causes for the decline of that culture. For the role of natural factors no valid evidence corresponding with the archaeological evidence is available. Natural factors do provide a challenge to human societies but it is their response which really matters in the growth or decline of a culture. The primacy of the socio-economic factors cannot be overruled. Similarly, external movements or invasions are effects of the internal weakening of societies and cultures rather than its causes. Agricultural efficiency declined due to floods or desiccation because of the shifting of the courses of the Indus, the Sutlej, the Sarasvati and the Drishadvati. Archaeological evidences indicate the drying up of lower Sarasvati before the arrival of PGW people who settled right in the flood plain in Haryana and Rajasthan.

Bhan also discusses distortions while dealing with the problem of periodisation in archaeology. The various nomenclatures 'Harappan' 'Early Harappan', 'Late Harappan' 'Chalcolithic Age' or 'Iron Age' do not indicate the precise connotation to which these terms have been used. He very rightly points out that it is not merely the metallurgical knowledge as the application of the specific types of tool-technology in the process of production which matters in giving a distinctive form to social development. He is also critical of unscientific and unhistorical approach of some archaeologists and Indologists that identifies the Indus civilisation with the Aryans. Whether it is a question of periodisation of specific culture formations or a study of relationship and comparison between different culture formations our analysis of the available archaeological evidence is likely to be defective and we may continue to arrive at faulty conclusion in the absence of a scientific historical approach based on time and space corelationship of the entire cultural data, including the correlation between its historical stages. Suraj Bhan, therefore, designates the pre-Harappan culture as representing a transitional stage in the growth of urbanisation and Harappan civilisation.

The population of the new people represented by PGW culture was maximum in the Sarasvati and the Yamuna valleys. It shows that these people moved into Haryana from Northern Panjab and/or along the Sarasvati valley. Except Bhagwanpura, no PGW site has been properly excavated. It was at this site, correlation between the post-Harappan and these new people was established. The knowledge of iron and glass technology, agriculture and cattle keeping and the manufacture of thin wheel-made fine grey pottery were the distinguishing features of the new people. They were thus in transition stage between tribal and a class-based society, centralised state and urbanisation. Suraj Bhan also discusses the problems of correlation between the PGW and Aryans and agrees with R.S. Sharma that the elements of the culture of the later-Vedic texts, namely, the use of iron and glass, stable agrarian society, cultivation of barley, wheat and rice, domestication of horse, cattle, sheep and goat, and the Varna based social stratification corresponds with those of PGW culture (about 258 sites of this culture have been brought to light in Haryana). Suraj Bhan carries his survey further to the historical period to the three phased NBP Ware culture on the basis of archaeological evidence gathered from Taxila, Ropar, Sugh, Agroha, Autha, Hat and Rohtak. In the first phase (*c.* 500-400 B.C.) NBP is introduced into the last stage of PGW culture; the second phase (*c.* 400-200 B.C.) marks the disappearance of the PGW and the introduction of unpainted Grey Ware and Red Ware, burnt brick structures, Brahmi script, punchmarked coins, profusion of terracotta and iron objects; the third phase (*c.* 200-100 B.C.) introduces Indo-Greek and tribal coins, rise of new towns such as Theh, Polar, Rohtak, Naurangabad with fortified settlements. It marks the diffusion of iron technology on large scale, artificial irrigation during NBP period, expansion of peasant communities and then lastly, the rise of several urban administrative centres like Indraprastha, Soneprastha, Rohitaka, Dhulkot, Meham, Naurangabad, Hansi, Jind and Sirsa. This is how Suraj Bhan reconstructs the history of the various phases of the growth of ancient Panjab with the application of a sound historical methodology. This is not to under-estimate the work done by other archaeologists like Y.D. Sharma, R.S. Bisht, G.C. Mahapatra which has its own importance but it is at the interpretational level where Suraj Bhan bases his investigations basically on socio-economic formations, his mark is distinctively felt. It may not be an exaggeration if I say that what Kosambi and R.S. Sharma have been doing in the field of history, Bhan is following in archaeology, particularly in those early periods of our historical growth where not much light is coming from the literary evidence which has its limitations.

Our historiographical survey of the trends in the Panjab comes to a close now. I have chosen a few representative historians and archaeologist for my analysis of the problem because their writings have a special bearing on it. No comprehensive history of ancient Panjab has been written so far, and in the general histories of India the region of our concern has not met with specific treatment. V.A. Smith represents the imperial school and Buddha Prakash belongs to the traditional school so far his writings are based primarily on the study of literary evidence and even if there is reference to the archaeological material it is by way of finding corroborative evidence and does not show any scientific approach due to his lack of specialised training involved in the latter discipline. Romila Thapar and Lallanji Gopal represent the rational school of historians of London, founded by the late A.L. Basham. Although accepting the fundamental proposition of Marx that economic factors play vital role in the historical growth, these two have developed independent lines of inquiry particularly on the socio-economic aspects of their respective studies. D.D. Kosambi, R.S. Sharma and Suraj Bhan reveal in their studies the influence of Marxism but they too do not display any commitment to ideology like the official Marxist school of historians for they use Marxism as a 'tool of analysis' and not a 'substitute of thinking'. For an analytical study of the socio-economic formations reference to Marxism is inevitable because of the very scientific nature of its fundamental proposition.

And finally, if the function of a historian as defined by E.H. Carr is "to master and understand the past as a key to the understanding of the present" then we have to undertake the historical reconstruction of our region on an altogether different line. We shall have to examine and explain all those factors which led the people towards progress and also those which brought their retardation and decline. In this process of investigation our approach cannot afford to be traditional, nationalistic or merely political for it has to take a serious note of socio-economic basis of culture formations. It would then become a reconstruction of the various facets of the life of the people, of their aspirations, achievements and failures, in fact, a study of their entire existence.

Select Bibliography

Basham, A.L., "Modern Historians of Ancient India" in *Historians of India, Pakistan and Ceylon* (ed.) C.H. Philips, Oxford, 1961.

Buddha Prakash, Presidential Address (Ancient Section), Panjab History Conference, 1965.

—, *Political and Social Movements in Ancient Panjab* (Delhi, 1963).

—, *Rigveda and the Indus Civilization* (Hoshiarpur, 1966).

—, *Glimpses of Ancient Panjab* (Patiala, 1966).

—, *Hariyana Through the Ages* (Kurukshetra, 1967).

—, *Evolution of Heroic Tradition in Ancient Panjab* (Patiala,1971).

Gopal, S. and Thapar, Romila (ed.), *Problems of Historical Writing in India,* The India International Centre, New Delhi, 1963.

Jha, D.N. "D.D. Kosambi" in *Historians and Historiography in Modern India,* (ed.) S.P. Sen (Calcutta, 1973).

Kosambi, D.D., *An Introduction to the Study of Indian History* (Bombay, 1956).

—, *The Culture and Civilization of Ancient India in Historical Outline* (London, 1965).

Lallanji Gopal, Presidential Address (Ancient Section), Panjab History Conference, 1978.

Phadke, H.A., "Literary Sources on the Historical Geography of Ancient Panjab" in *Sources of the History of India,* Vol.V, Calcutta.

—, "'Haryana, the Landmarks in Historical Growth", *Indological Studies,* (ed.) Devendra Handa (Delhi,1987).

—, *History of Kurukshetra* (Jointly with V.N. Datta) (Kurukshetra, 1984).

—, *Hariyana: Ancient and Medieval,* (Delhi, 1990).

—, Ancient Sections (Early History and Archaeology).

—, Haryana State and District Gazetteers (Jind, Ambala, Hisar, Sirsa, Sonepat, Mahendragarh, Kurukshetra and Rohtak) (New Series).

Raychaudhuri, H.C., *Political History of Ancient India,* 6th edn. (Calcutta, 1953)

—, *Studies in Indian Antiquities* (Calcutta, 1958).

Sarvapalli, Radhakrishnan (ed.), *Indian Philosophy*, Vol. I, 1956.

—, *History of Philosophy, Eastern and Western* Vol. I,"The Upanishadas" by T.M.P. Mahadevan, pp. 56-7 London, George Allan and Unwin Ltd., 1957.

Sharma, R.S., *Indian Feudalism*, Macmillan India Limited, 1980.

—, *Material Culture and Social Formations in Ancient India*, Macmillan India Limited, 1985 (Reprint).

Singh, Fauja and Joshi, L.M. (ed.), *History of Panjab*, Vol. I and II (Patiala, 1977).

Sircar, D.C., "Ancient Geography of the Punjab" in *History of the Punjab* (ed.) L.M. Joshi, Vol.I (Patiala, 1977).

Smith, V.A., *The Early History of India*, Oxford, 1924.
—, *The Oxford History of India*, Oxford, 1958.
Suraj Bhan, Presidential Address (Ancient Section), Panjab History Conference, 1985.
—, Presidential Address (Archaeology Section) Indian History Congress, Srinagar, 1986.
—, "Emergence of Urbanization and its Decline in Proto-Historical Period: A Plea for Historical Approach".
—, "Production Techniques and Social Formations in Vedic and Post-Vedic Times" Review article based on R.S. Sharma, *Material Culture and Social Formations in Ancient India, The Indian Historical Review,* Vol. XI, 1988.
Thapar, Romesh (ed.), "Past and Present", *Seminar*, November, 1962.
Thapar, Romila, Presidential Address (Ancient Section), "The Scope and Significance of Regional History" Panjab History Conference, 1976; *Ancient Indian Social History,* Delhi, 1978.

8

National Integration: The Historical and Philosophical View

While exposing the fundamental unity of India our pioneer historians laid specific stress on the influence of geographical factors on her history and culture.[1] It was but natural, for they had to combat the western view highlighting the factors of our disintegration for justification of the British rule over India. Historical growth of a people does not depend on geo-political factors alone. It rests basically on the consciousness of man of his conditions which induce him to device means to simplify the forces of nature for the betterment of life. It is perhaps instinctive in human beings to develop emotional attachment to the place of their long association, the precious memory of which they carry to the last moments of their life. An understanding of the socio-economic foundations of this aspect of human existence would perhaps better explain the role of geographical factors in the integration of a people.[2]

Indian sub-continent, broadly consisting of three distinct physiographic divisions, namely, the North, the Deccan and the South, in course of historical growth, gave birth to various regional, linguistic and political identities. These identities preserved in very old persisting literary and folk traditions, give dynamism to regional and historical memories to this day

('Through the Ages' histories of different regions best illustrate this).[3] Nevertheless, it may be pointed out that these identities would become meaningless if divorced from their relevance to the historical growth of the whole nation. It should also be remembered that the geographical conditions of India closed her to the outside world for long and gave her a peculiar character deeply affecting the course of the development of her social structure.[4]

Except under the Mauryas and the Mughals, larger portion of India was never brought under one sceptre. The establishment of the British rule, with its introduction of the systems of transport, means of communication, industrial growth and other such measures already known to the western world, succeeded for the first time, in bringing the whole of India under single administrative control. India never witnessed such political, and administrative uniformity before, but neither did India have at any time in her long history fixed political divisions into distinct regions as she had during the British rule. Her disunity was mainly due to dynastic rivalries and imperial ambitions of her rulers. However, there seems no doubt that India did possess some kind of a cultural unity as expressed in the concept of Bharatavarsha, in the uniformity of the spiritual and moral outlook of the people and in their common belief in the concepts of *karma*, *avatara*, *punarjanma* and *varnashrama*.[5] The institution of pilgrimage also worked for religious synthesis bringing peoples of distant regions together.[6] Despite this, it must also be admitted that some of our worst social evils - degraded position of women, untouchability and the rigid caste system, which have their roots in our past, have been major constraints in the process of the real integration of the Indian people. This contradiction of the Indian ethos - broad tolerance and freedom of thought on one hand, and narrow social form of behaviour on the other, rightly drew the attention of Pt. Nehru who considered social change as "an inevitable consequence of political and economic change, a necessary condition if we are to remain integrated human beings and integrated nation".[7]

Universal love, brotherhood and tolerance are indeed very noble ideas but one has to understand them in the context of Indian social development. The very fact that a great religious reformer like Buddha failed to act positively by not imposing upon his followers the duty of neglecting their castes in social relations and that Ashoka, the great Mauryan emperor, the medieval Bhakti saints and the nineteenth century religious and social reformers, had to stress time and again on tolerance and promotion of peaceful coexistence among various religious and social groups, bespeak of the socio-cultural and religious strains all through the ages. There seems to be same justification for R.G. Bhandarkar's lamentations that "India had no social and political revolution" though she did experience "religious revolution".[8] The earlier reform movements did not look upon the caste system as a social evil (as was done by the reformers of modern times) and hence, they remained content only with some change in the religious and moral spheres. But there is no doubt that these movements did an excellent service by carrying the common cultural heritage to the masses through the medium of popular languages. In this process the regional languages became highly developed, and in course of time, became the vehicles of the Indian freedom struggle. In India, mass cultural participation was regulated by the caste system and perhaps this factor considerably helped preserving some kind of cultural unity among the people.

It was perhaps the common bondage which taught the Indians their first lesson in the direction of unification. And the common feeling of hatred for the foreign rule led to the rise of nationalism which, in course of time, took the form of a movement for the liberation of the whole Indian people. With the attainment of independence, were also brought to surface centrifugal forces (so far remained suppressed due to the rising tide of nationalism), in various forms – regionalism, linguism, communalism and casteism. Their worst manifestation in recent times is perhaps the 'sons of the soil' doctrine, which although has its origin in the economic backwardness of the people and the unemployment of the educated, goes contrary to the fundamental rights guaranteed by the constitution to all citizens and undermines administrative efficiency. The situation is further aggravated by politicians who exploit the regional feelings to meet their own narrow ends.[9]

That these forces have now reached to a dangerous extent can be gathered from the nature and form of the agitation over the implementation of the Mandal Commission Report on the job reservations for the backward classes. This explains why Gandhiji gave so much stress on 'spiritual corrective' and 'regeneration of the individual' instead of collective action for effecting social change.[10] 'Fratricide', warned V.K. Krishna Menon, "is a part of our national heritage. I fear that we do not yet realise the danger that lies ahead in this aspect of our modern being." And Nehru, who regarded "fostering the unity of India as his profession", was well aware of the "sectional interests eating its very roots". In his address to the National Integration Conference (New Delhi, 1961) he very correctly stressed the need of removing social and economic backwardness of the people. The question of integration covered our entire existence, particularly the system of education which is supposed to offer proper training to the individual, he pointed out.[11] The split personality of India – that is, wide gap between our professions and practice, our ideals of peace, non-violence, tolerance and philosophic detachment even in the midst of action, as they stood in sharp contrast to the lower plane of our behaviour, degrading us as individuals and as a community, was the subject of his deepest concern.[12] That it strained his mind even towards the close of his life becomes evident from his will, one of the most precious historical documents of this century. Although fully aware of the devastating effects of the working of the forces of disintegration, Nehru earnestly desired preservation of the humanitarian and beneficial elements of our past tradition. He wrote[13]:

> And though I have discarded much of the past tradition and custom, and am anxious that India should rid herself of all shackles that bind and constrain her and divide her people and suppress vast numbers of them, to prevent free development of the body and the spirit; though I seek all this, yet I do not wish to cut myself off from the past completely. I am proud of that great inheritance that has been and is, ours, and I am conscious that I too, like all of us, am a link in that unbroken chain which goes back to the dawn of history in the immemorial past of India.

So far we have discussed integration in political and social spheres. There is still a different type of integration, which, although glimpsed for the first time in Indian philosophical thought, has its fuller exposition in recent times in the discourses of J. Krishnamurti. In its clarity and profundity Krishnamurti's perception of the fundamental human problem stands in close comparison to that found in the discourses of Socrates and Buddha and in the writings of Bertrand Russell in modern times. The basic idea of his teachings, as very aptly pointed out by Aldous Huxley, is that for individual the central human problem can be solved in only one way – for and by himself; and that is through self-knowledge, not through belief in someone else's symbols, that a man comes to the eternal reality, in which his being is grounded. Collective solutions, to which so many so desperately pin their faith are never adequate.[14]

The real meaning of integration, according to this view, cannot be fully grasped unless the relationship between individual and society is properly understood. Society exists for the individual, to give him freedom, to awaken highest intelligence. This intelligence should in no way be regarded as mere cultivation of a technique or of knowledge; nor is it a cumulative result. It is the manifestation of that creative reality which gives freedom from all progressive achievements and success. Intelligence is thus neither static nor could it be copied, standardised or taught, it is to be discovered only in freedom. This freedom can never be sought in any collective action. The conflict between the individual and the society is nothing but the reflection of the inner conflict between that which is living and that which is static.[15] In view of this a clear distinction between a citizen and the individual needs to be made. The state and the society are not concerned with the inner man but only with the outer man, the citizen. "A good citizen is not necessarily a good man; but a good man is bound to be a right citizen" says Krishnamurti. State cannot but be against the goodman, the man of highest intelligence who is not bound to any condition. The state sacrifices the individual for the citizen, the present for the future. But to the intelligent man the present is of highest importance, the now and not the tomorrow.[16] With a remarkable clarity Krishnamurti further explains the results which follow such a perception. He writes:[17]

> The understanding of what *is* brings about transformation in the immediate present. It is this transformation that is of supreme importance; and not how to reconcile the citizen with the man. When this transformation takes place, the conflict between man and citizen ceases.

Fundamental change in the society, therefore, must begin with inner psychological transformation of the individual, that is making him aware of the various ways of disintegration conflict, discontent, competition, striving and so on, at all levels of our existence. "Is it the ideal", asks Krishnamurti, "that makes us struggle to become *that* when we are *this*?"[18] Ideas, conclusions, explanations – all prevent understanding for these are nothing but projections of the mind. Belief in any form, whether religious, economic or social, separates man from man, it does not unite people.[19] In order to understand the nature of disintegrating society Krishnamurti suggests negative investigation, that is not with a positive formula or a conclusion.[20] Imitation and disintegration go together. To be creative we must have freedom from authority. "In moments of creativeness there is no repetition. Such moments are always new, fresh, creative and happy".[21]

Even discipline in the sense of conformity, resistance, or opposition may be regarded as one of the factors of disintegration. Fear is the basis of all discipline. Fear of being insecure makes for conformity both outward and inward. Discipline in any form can never bring freedom from fear, it has to be observed, studied and understood.[22] The process of disintegration can be observed in the working of our system of education, social structure and religious institutions based on imitative and fixed formulas. So long as state controls education, fear and discipline through punishment and rewards shall always remain. The state is interested in mass produced citizens, it prefers mass education. The ruling class does not want discontent, for their position would soon be untenable.[23] The entire process of becoming, of making efforts to change 'what is' into 'what should be' leads to an illusion. And that which brings illusion cannot but be the disintegration factor. 'Integration', says Krishnamurti, "is neither the action of will, nor it is the process of becoming integrated. It is not a goal, an end, but a state of being, it is a living thing. It is a state of complete attention. When disintegration is not, when there is no conflict, no struggle to become, only then is there the being of the whole, the complete".[24]

To the world community, presently passing through this very process of disintegration, internal as well as external, Krishnamurti's message is invaluable. The problem of integration is not thus confined to India alone. It has assumed global relevance.

Notes

1. R.K. Mookerji, *Fundamental Unity of India*, Calcutta, 1913.
2. H.A. Phadke, "Trends in the Historiography of Panjab", Panjab History Conference, Patiala, 1988, Proceedings.
3. Selig S. Harrison, *India: The Most Dangerous Decades*, Oxford, 1960; K.M. Panikkar, *Geographical Factors in Indian History*, Bombay, 1955; K.A. Nilakantha Shastri, *Factors in Indian History*, Waltair, 1949; *Seminar*, Delhi, 1962.
4. Nehru's Foreword to Ramdhari Singh Dinkar's *Samskriti ke Chara Adhyaya*, 30 September, 1955.
5. V.S. Agrawala, *Bharata Ki Maulika Ekata*, Bharati Bhandar, Allahabad, 1954; R.N. Misra, "A Perspective of Integration" *Problems of Indian Historiography*, (ed.) Devahuti, Delhi, 1979, pp.29-34.
6. R.N. Misra, *op.cit.*
7. H.A. Phadke, "Nehru's Rationalism", All India Radio, Rohtak, 11 October, 1980.
8. R.G. Bhandarkar, *Collected Works*, Poona, II, pp.478-79.
9. H.A. Phadke, "Sons of the Soil Doctrine and the National Mainstream", All India Radio, Rohtak, 15 July, 1980.
10. *Seminar*, February, 1988.
11. *Nehru's Vision*, Haryana Sahitya Akademy, Chandigarh, 1989, pp.65-66.
12. H.A. Phadke, *op.cit.*
13. *Seminar*, July, 1964, pp.49-50.
14. J. Krishnamurti, *The First and Last Freedom*, London, 1972, Foreword by Aldous Huxly, pp.11-12.
15. J. Krishnamurti, *Commentaries on Living*, First Series, London, 1976 ("The Individual and Society", pp.30-31.)
16. *Ibid.*, p.31-2.
17. *Ibid.*, p.32.
18. *Ibid.*, pp.195-96.
19. *The First and Last Freedom*, p.38.
20. *Ibid.*, pp.39-40.
21. *Ibid.*, pp.40-41.
22. *Commentaries*, Second Series, pp.48-49 ('Education and Integration').
23. *Ibid.*, p.49.
24. *Ibid.*, I. p.197; II, p.57.

9

Nehru's Rationalism

Rationalism denotes a tendency to demand for a reasonable explanation of prevailing beliefs, customs and institutions in scientific terms; Jawaharlal Nehru was the symbol of Indian rational humanistic thought in modern times. Born in an aristocratic liberal family, he was influenced in his early life by theosophy, and later by the rationalist thought which he imbibed at Cambridge. He was the promoter of 'scientific humanism', a concept governed by a practical idealism having "humanity its god and social service its religion". To understand this, one has to peep into the totality of Nehru's life and work, his answers to such metaphysical questions as the existence of God and meaning of religion as also his reflections on the real problems of his times - education, communalism, caste, untouchability, dogmatism, necessity of scientific attitude and lack of proper concept of history.

Although Nehru did not believe in the existence of God, his strict adherence to goodness and truth made him, as rightly put by Gandhi, "nearer to God than many who profess to be His worshippers". Too much reliance on supernatural factors according to him, "leads to a loss of self-reliance in man and to a blunting of his capacity and creative ability". But, at the same time, he thinks it desirable to have faith in something which he called 'a creative life-giving force', or a 'vital energy inherent in matter' which has a capacity for change and growth, giving meaning and purpose to life. Any idea of a personal god seemed odd to him.

It was again his scientific approach which made him sceptical to religion. The study of world civilisations made him realise that religion satisfied some deeply felt inner needs of human nature. Nehru strongly favoured the application of scientific method even for the study of religious experience. Metaphysical and philosophical questions such as future life, soul or incarnation and *karma* only aroused his intellectual curiosity but in no way affected his life or his convictions. He was shocked at Gandhi's remark that the Bihar earthquake (1934) "had been a punishment for the sins of untouchability". Anything more opposed to the scientific outlook than this he considered difficult to imagine. The preconceived notions in religion shut our eyes to the realities of life and therefore Nehru found it difficult to enter into any discussion with the convinced believers of any creed. To Nehru, religion denotes 'inner development' of the individual of which the 'outward change' was nothing but a projection, both acting and reacting on each other. Although accepting that there may be exceptional individuals who might rise above their conditions of life, yet it is very difficult for larger groups or nations who are subject to political and economic exploitation. Religion as it is practised in India, Nehru compared with the old man of the sea which has "broken our backs and stunted and almost killed all originality of thought". He asks, "Faith in progress, in cause, in human goodness and human destiny, are they not really allied to faith in a Providence?"

The defective system of our education based on tradition, ignorance and refusal to think upset Nehru. For a healthy development of our body and mind, he strongly recommended the study of Bertrand Rusell's ideas on education. An advocate of Hindustani, he considered the case of English as the lingua franca of India, a fantastic conception having no relation with the problem of mass education and culture. He was equally distressed at the rise of communalism in India, a question which could be settled only by mutual understanding or by "coldly reasoned tolerance" as he put it, but he was fully aware of a "third party in control playing off one group against another".

Thus opposed to all sort of irrationalism, Nehru places his complete reliance on truth and science. The concept of the truth of Nehru is something dynamic and not static, for it is in consonance with his ideas on science. "It is the scientific approach", he says, "the adventurous and yet critical temper of science, the search for truth and new knowledge, the refusal to accept anything without testing and trial, the capacity to change previous conclusions in the face of new evidence, the reliance on observed fact and not on preconceived theory, the hard discipline of the mind – all this is necessary, not merely for the application of science but for life and the solution of its many problems".

Although critical of the treatment of Marx's writings as revealed religion, and use of violence even in normal times in Russia, Nehru was a great admirer of Marx's insight into social phenomenon and the scientific method which he adopted. Nehru is perfectly right while contending that this is the only scientific method which helps in understanding the past and the present and this explains why "the most revealing and keen analysis of the changes that are taking place today come from the Marxist writers". In its absence of dogmatism and in its scientific approach leading to action lies the whole value of Marxism. Viewed in this light, Nehru's ideas on social and political change become meaningful. "Good of a nation or of mankind". he says, "must not be held up because some people who profit by the existing order object to the change. If political and social institutions stand in the way of such a change, they have to be removed".

His concept of history differs from that of the nineteenth century, regarding history to be 'a string of odd facts'. He explains history as "the study of the interaction of various forces in which the economic predominates". Nehru's approach to history is an approach to understand life where "past becomes something that leads up to the present, the moment of action, the future something that flows from it; and all three, are inextricably intertwined and interrelated". He was influenced by Bury's 'Idea of Progress' which explained history in terms of the growth and advance of man through the ages. The geographical conditions of India which closed her to the outside world for long gave her a peculiar character deeply affecting the course of the development of her social structure (the introduction of caste system and untouchability for instance, which were unknown to the contemporary world). This split personality of India – broad tolerance and freedom of thought on one hand, and narrow social form of behaviour on the other, were the themes of his deepest concern. He came closer to the political thought of Justice Ranade when he considered social change as an inevitable consequence of political and economic change, a necessary condition if we are to remain integrated human beings and an integrated nation. Political change and industrial progress are not possible without change in the social structure.

Nehru remained a rational humanist throughout his life. Its best testimonial is perhaps his own will, one of the most precious national documents of this century. Dedicated with profound gratitude to Mother India and her sons, it reads:

> My desire to have handful of my ashes thrown into Ganga has no religious significance. Ganga has been to me a symbol and a memory of the past of India, running into the present, and flowing on to the great ocean of the future (an interesting observation for the modern historiographer for his 'unending dialogue between the past, present and the future').

> And though I have discarded much of past tradition and custom and am anxious that India should get rid herself of all shackles that bind and constrain her and divide her

people, yet I do not wish to cut myself off from the past completely ... I am conscious that I too, like all of us, am a link in that unbroken chain which goes back to the dawn of history in the immemorial past of India.

Select Bibliography

Chalapathi Rau, M., *Jawaharlal Nehru: Life and Work*, New Delhi, 1966.
Das, M.N., *The Political Philosophy of Jawaharlal Nehru*, London, 1961.
Datta, V.N. and Cleghorn, B., *The Nationalist Muslim and Indian Politics*, Macmillan, 1974.
Jawaharlal Nehru, *Glimpses of World History*, Indian Edition, 1949.
—, *The Discovery of India*, London, 1960.
—, *An Autobiography*, Indian Edition, 1962.
Seminar, "Jawaharlal Nehru", "Nehru and the Ism", July and November, 1964.
The Century, Special, January, 1965.

II

Social and Intellectual Movements in Maharashtra (Nineteenth Century)

The impact of the West and the consequent growth of the intellectual movement in India have drawn considerable attention of scholars in modern times. In Western India, it was marked by reforms in social, religious, educational and judicial spheres. Towards this end, the beginning was made by Mountstuart Elphinstone, the first Governor of the Bombay Presidency (1819-1827) who considered administrative reforms as essential for the moral regeneration of the Indians and for the growth of scientific spirit among them. This programme of reform was taken up further by such eminent Indians as Bal Shastri Jambhekar, R.G. Bhandarkar, V.N. Mandlik, M.G. Ranade, K.T. Telang and, N.M. Paramanand - all Elphinstonians and V.S. Pandit, G.H. Deshmukh, Jyotiba Phule and G.G. Agarkar of the Pune Reformist school. A modest attempt has been made in the following pages to focus attention on the intellectual system of these luminaries so as to understand their perception and analysis of our social, cultural and political maladies which were at the very root of our national decline.

It may also be mentioned here that the nomenclature Western India, has been used in the text to denote the area covered by Western Maharashtra. The former was accepted by many a scholar working on the subject. However, the designation *Ajakalacha* Maharashtra, suggested for the first time by Prabhakar Padhye and S.R. Tikekar, admirably suits the subject-matter of the present study.

10

Mountstuart Elphinstone and the Growth of Indological Consciousness in Western India

Indological consciousness came to India as a direct consequence of the educational and administrative policy of the early British rulers. Although concerned primary with the consolidation of the British rule, these early administrator-historians widely differed in their emphasis and treatment of the history and culture of the Indian people.[1] One school of thought condemned institutions of the Hindus, their administration of justice and principles of law and found nothing impressive about their contributions to art, literature and science; while to the other, the Hindu civilisation represented an advanced stage of development.[2] Mountstuart Elphinstone, the Governor of the Bombay Presidency (1819-1827), was the foremost exponent of the latter school of thought in western India. Elphinstone considered improvement in the educational system as essential for the moral regeneration of the Indians and his administrative reforms showed no trace of bias but rather a sympathetic understanding of the subjects over which he ruled.

Elphinstone's famous *Minute on Education* reflects his wisdom, insight and deep sympathy for the Indians. Considering western system of education as indispensable to the growth of scientific spirit among the natives he defined a policy of state initiative and control in education, stressed the need of cooperation between the state and private efforts and a system of grant-in-aid.[3] He was of the view that the government should disassociate from all religious institutions or any education which had a religious bias. The efforts of Christian missionaries he considered as "the alarm to warn the Brahmins of the approaching danger" and any effort at conversion as "spelling not only the ruin of the plan of education but the dissolution of the empire".[4] In a letter to Captain George Jervis he explains the aim of education as "the redemption of human beings from gross mental darkness and unhappiness, an object which must touch every heart endowed with the slightest sense of benevolence".

Although the Brahmanical learning was regarded unprofitable, Elphinstone was still in favour of its continuance, possibly also due to the fact that a Brahmin rule was overthrown and a need was urgently felt to pacify that community which was the chief beneficiary under the previous educational system. He wrote:[5]

> Their (of the Brahmins) learning may have been obscure and degenerate, but it bore some affinity to real science into which it might in time have been improved. They (the Brahmins) were not perhaps much inferior to those monks among whom the seeds of European learning were long kept alive and their extinction, if it did not occasion the loss of much present wisdom, would have cut off all hopes for the future.

Elphinstone was against the total abandonment of the purely Hindu part of the course of studies which to him was a preposterous way of adding to the intellectual treasures of the nation to begin by destroying its indigenous literature. His memorandum on the Poona College further reveals his anxiety for the promotion of indigenous learning.[6] In his report submitted to the Bengal Government in 1819 concerning conquered Peshwa territories, he proposed to the government to sanction the grant of two lacs of rupees in continuation of the Peshwa tradition of the Dakshina and afterwards conceded with Rs.50,000 for the creation of Dakshina fellowships.[7] Elphinstone effected a change in the previous practice by giving grants not for divinity but for useful learning including the promotion of oriental studies. His benevolent measures were extended also to the field of social regeneration and judicial reforms. The suggestions he made in favour of the abolition of the evil social customs like the burning of the widows, infanticide, slavery and for the continuation of the village panchayats disclose his understanding of the urgent need of the reform of Indian social and judicial system.[8] He made efforts to compile a complete and consistent code (known after him as the Elphinstone Code) from the mass of written law and the fragments of tradition and hence was rightly held as the pioneer of the rule of law in Western India.[9] Elphinstone was aware that in India the ties of religion were stronger than law and therefore purification of the tenets of the natives was essential for enlightening them on such matters. Although conscious of the dangers involved in his liberal policy of imparting western education to the natives, he was in no way prepared to abandon it. With a prophetic vision he explained his point of view to James Lake. He wrote:[10]

> We are educating the natives. Here it is even more important and more hazardous experiment ... it will be better for us to lose the country by the effects of our liberality than keep it like Dutchmen or Spaniards, not that I think the immediate danger of our losing the country increased by education ...but there can be no doubt that when the natives get more extended notions they will

expect, first a share of their own government and then the whole.

The renaissance which was witnessed in Western India as a result of the new education and administrative policy of Elphinstone also led to the discovery of antiquities and ancient literature of India by a band of scholars towards which the beginning was already made in 1804 by Sir James Mackintosh with the foundation of the Literary Society of Bombay. It was this society which was utilised by Elphinstone for his educational programme.[11] The library of the Bombay branch of the Royal Asiatic Society became the source of inspiration to the members of the literary society and in due course many distinguished oriental scholars came to be ranked amongst its members.[12] Among the members of the society were such prominent citizens like Jagannath Sankarshett whose advice Elphinstone sought in framing his educational scheme.[13]

The fundamental ideas which inspired Elphinstone are reflected in his journals, letters and historical works – the basic source material for an understanding of his training, method and intellectual system. His long stay for more than thirty years in India, his association with prominent Indians, knowledge of Persian and Hindustani and extensive travels provided him with knowledge of the local conditions. He had visited a number of historical places. The massive, hoary and venerable beauty of the Kailash temple and the solemnity and gloomy magnificence of the Karle Caves particularly struck him with wonder and admiration and made him reflect on the richness and variety of the ancient civilisation of India.[14] He had played a major role in the process of the consolidation of the British rule in India and being a foreigner "the possibilities of exercising detachment were greater for him than those of a local historian".

Elphinstone's *The History of India* (The Hindu and Muhammadan Periods) was published in 1841. Another volume on the *Rise of British Power in the East* he could not complete for he realised that it is not possible for him to compete in this field with either Mill or Macaulay. Perhaps he was too modest to be confident. Presenting his work by way of an introduction to the growth of man's mind and culture, he makes his style "condensed and animated and the reflections striking and profound".

In his historical narrative Elphinstone displays a sympathetic understanding of Indian history and culture. Having observed the variations in human nature all over the world he set his object as to merely describe it rather than enter into value judgements. History to him was an accurate and authentic narrative of the past and therefore should be based on a scientific study of the evidence and the inference thus drawn should be free from any bias or any preconceived notion. He was aware that in history there can be no finality and there shall always remain scope for revision, modification and reinterpretation.[15] A real history of India cannot be written without direct contact with the Indian situation, he believed. Unlike Mill whose writings provoked Indian historians to challenge western attacks on Indian culture, Elphinstone followed a really constructive and more humane approach providing thereby a proper perspective to the new generation of Indian scholars in the formidable task of reconstructing their past.

Elphinstone makes full use of the then available source-material – the ancient Hindu texts, the works of Colebrooke, Wilson, Hamilton, Buchanan, Ward, Tod, Malcolm, Kennedy, the *Asiatic Researches* and the *Transactions of the Royal Asiatic Society.* He provides a chronological framework but does not attempt reconstruction of the political history of ancient India; perhaps it was too early for him to do so in the absence of adequate historical evidence. He, therefore, concerns himself mainly with the evaluation of the cultural achievements of the Hindus, provides details on their society, religion, literature, philosophy, arts and sciences, manners and customs, trade and commerce and India's overseas trade and thus lays the foundation for future extensive researches in the field.

In his studies, Elphinstone found ancient Indian institutions in an advanced stage of development and the artistic achievements though 'in a simple state' yet 'far from being rude'. According to him the Ramayana and the Mahabharata contained many spirited poetical passages and that the Indians were far advanced in their original contribution to algebra, and in arithmetic they were distinguished by their invention of the decimal notation. The institution of caste although an impediment in the growth of the feeling of nationality, in India it did not have that great impact as several European writers liked us to believe. Elphinstone presents a very useful and fairly detailed account of the social system, the account of the classical writers on India, revenue system but more systematic and appreciative is the section dealing with Hindu religions. He separates facts from mythology, does not study the state of Hindu society by western standards, but evaluates it in the context of its conditioning circumstances. He takes into account the process of social change, offers explanations and is full of admiration for the antiquity and vitality of the Hindu civilisation.[16] The medieval portion of this work is based on English translations of the original Persian texts.[17] It is a study of political history on dynastic pattern and concerns very little with culture, society and economic activities.

The work was intended to evoke interest of the English readers who were little aware of the ancient and medieval periods of Indian history. A valuable source for those seeking information on the early history of India, the work indeed fulfilled expectations of its author. Explaining Elphistone's difficulties in undertaking this work, his biographer T.E. Colebrooke wrote:[18]

> The history of race so deficient in historical records as the Hindoos resolves itself into a series of antiquarian discussions and that of the Mohammedan period, important as it is in its bearing on Modern History became insipid from

the sameness of revolutions which it records. The manner in which Elphinstone overcame these disadvantages ensured its success.

Cowell said:[19]

> The charm of the book is the spirit of genuine, hearty sympathy with and appreciation of, the native character, which runs through the whole, and the absence of which is one of the main blemishes of Mr. Mill's eloquent work.

Elphinstone not only wrote himself but inspired a number of his colleagues who were engaged in similar pursuits. Grant Duff completed his two volumes on 'A History of the Marathas' by 1825. Erskine translated the Memoirs of Babur from Persian while James Tod's *The Annals and Antiquities of Rajasthan* created a stir in the then academic circle.

Elphinstone's attention was also drawn towards epigraphy, an important branch of indological studies. He was particularly anxious about the proper study and preservation of ancient inscriptions. A number of his letters written to Erskine are devoted to this subject.[20] He inspired certain of his friends to collect inscriptions from various parts of India. It was a scholarly movement and Elphinstone wished Erskine to lead it. To the latter he wrote:[21]

> Norris in Cutch, Barnell in Kattywar, Miles on the North-West Frontier, Grant at Sattara etc. would probably have zeal enough for this but it is necessary, in the first place, to have some instructions drawn out to show what sort of inscriptions are desirable and what errors to guard against in transcribing them – and in the second, it is necessary that somebody should arrange them when they arrive and point out, in what places the search should be pursued....

The task of making an explanatory catalogue was entrusted to Walter; Kennedy was to undertake the correspondence while Erskine was to be in-charge of the whole scheme including selection of inscriptions for translations and their publications.[22] Elphinstone's trust in Erskine was indeed well placed. What a perfect judgement he had of the capabilities of his colleagues becomes clear from what Erskine wrote back to him. It reads:[23]

> Any work in prose, any letter, journal (if such a thing existed), history, geography, list of priests in a temple, in short any memorial whatever would have its use. Songs and poems have a better chance to be preserved and are valuable documents, though in some particulars less valuable than prose writing.

Erskine preferred inscriptions of unknown character and those of two hundred years old and upwards, in whatever Indian character, he considered of special importance particularly in assisting the decipherment of the unknown scripts. He was not unmindful of the use of Jaina or heretical inscriptions for historical study and included in the list of desiderata coins also, the branch of study which was then not even in initial stages in India.

Elphinstone was for perfection in copying of inscriptions so as to make it useful for historical study. The decipherment of ancient scripts drew his attention particularly those he found in the caves he visited, and felt that this would be very valuable for the study of the conditions of south and west India before the establishment of *brahmins* and *shanscrit*.[24] Elphinstone, a very keen observer as he was, could distinguish between the script of one inscription from other. On the copies of the Carle Cave Inscription which he sent to Erskine for decipherment he remarked:[25]

> I have no doubt that you will be struck with the resemblance between them and the inscriptions copied from Allahabad and Delhi published in the volume of the Asiatic Researches but on comparison, the characters will not be found the same.

In the task of decipherment the method which he preferred was from known to unknown scripts. In a letter to Capt. Caulfield in Indore he pointed out the importance of sculptural dedication of a temple or a cave for the understanding of the relationship between Brahmanism and Buddhism and which might possibly lead to deciphering of the unknown character in which so much of the religious history of South India appears to be.[26]

Because of the unhistorical character of the early Indian literature, Elphinstone puts more reliance on inscriptions for historical reconstruction. He instructed Capt. Caulfield for the guidance of those who were engaged in Malwa in the task of collection of inscriptions and information about languages spoken for forming a vocabulary. The latter was yet another field of interest of Elphinstone. Elphinstone had himself prepared scripts of different languages spoken in Nagpur but unfortunately this collection is lost.[27] He was fully aware of the difficulties in getting suitable persons with real interest in the work of arranging vocabularies and used to refer with regret to the work of Marshall who failed because of the lack of someone to carry on his work.[28]

The indological consciousness in Western India thus owes its beginning to the efforts of these early British officers who took a more favourable view of the Indian people and had a sympathetic understanding of their problems. And above them all stood Mountstuart Elphinstone, deeply concerned with tracing "the progress of improvement and of liberal ideas" among the Indian people.

Elphinstone could not stay here to see the full results of his enlightened policy, but there had never been any doubt about the profound impact it made on the intellectual life of Western India. This becomes evident from the tributes paid to him by the citizens of the Bombay Presidency at the time of his departure from India. Their address on this occasion not only shows awareness of his excellent works in the fields of education and learning but also their deep sense of gratitude as expressed in their determination to raise his permanent monument by collecting a fund for the foundation of professorships bearing his name.[29] It was decided that the said professorships would be held in the first instance by learned men from England until natives of the country were found perfectly competent to undertake that office.[30]

The sincere efforts of the citizens of the Bombay Presidency were ultimately realised when in 1834 the Elphinstone Institution was founded which in course of time developed into a nucleus of a great intellectual movement in Western India.[31] A. Orlebar and John Harkness were the earliest European professors of the institution who were joined by Bal Gangadhar Shastri Jambhekar as Assistant Professor, the first ever Indian to be appointed over that assignment and later Bhau Daji and R.G. Bhandarkar were also associated with teaching in that seat of learning. Elphinstone's original idea of creation of fellowships out of the Dakshina Fund for the promotion of indigenous learning was also realised. The director of public instruction E.I. Howard got the government to place the Dakshina Fund into his hands for the creation of fellowships called Dakshina Fellows.[32] This association of Indians with research and teaching proved to be very beneficial for they came closer to the European scholars, learnt from them their methodology and raised themselves to a position to interpret their own history and culture independently.

The indological consciousness in Western India evoked by the intellectual system and enlightened administrative measures of Mountstuart Elphinstone thus gave to the Bombay Presidency a position of premier importance in the field of Sanskrit and Oriental learning which drew the attention even of the great German Orientalist, Max Mueller who remarked:[33]

> The intellectual life of India at the present moment is full of interesting problems. A new race of men is growing up in India, ... with regard to what is of greatest interest to us their scholarship, it is true that the old school of Sanskrit scholars is dying out and much will die with it which we shall never recover; but a new and most promising school of Sanskrit students, educated by European Professors, is springing up, and they will, nay, to judge from recent controversies, they have already become more formidable rivals to our own scholars.... The essays of Dr. Bhau Daji on disputed points in Indian Archaeology and literature, are most valuable. The editions of Sanskrit texts published by Prof. Bhandarkar and Shankar Pandurang Pandit and others, need not fear comparison with the best work of European scholars.

Notes

1. S.N. Mukherjee, "Sir William Jones and British Attitudes to India", Cambridge, 1968, Introduction.
2. Mountstuart Elphinstone, *History of India: The Hindu and Muhammadan Periods*, with notes and additions by E.B. Cowell, London, 1935; James Mill, *The History of British India*, (ed.) by H.H. Wilson, London, 1858.
3. Sri T.E. Colebrooke, *Life of the Honourable Mountstuart Elphinstone*, 2 Vols, London, 1884, II, p. 151f; Elphinstone's Minute, December 13, 1823; J.S. Cotton, *Mountstuart Elphinstone*, Oxford, 1892; C.H. Philips (ed.), *Historians of India, Pakistan and Ceylon*, Oxford, 1961.
4. Colebrooke, op.cit., Vol.II, pp.156-62.

5. R.D. Choksey, *Mountstuart Elphinstone (The Indian Years 1796-1827)*, Popular Prakashan, Bombay, 1971, p.386; *Maharashtra Jivana*, ed. by G.B. Sardar, Poona, 1960, II, p.15.
6. Choksey, op.cit., p.387.
7. H. Sharp, *Selections from Educational Records*, Part I, Calcutta, 1920, p.198.
8. Colebrooke, op.cit., II, p.154; Choksey, op.cit., pp.422-37.
9. Ibid.
10. The letter dated 4th September, 1823 as quoted by Choksey, op.cit., pp. 396-97 fn. see also Colebrooke, op.cit., II, pp.159-60.
11. Choksey, op.cit., p.393.
12. Choksey, op.cit.
13. See Sir Bartle Frere's remark quoted by V.M. Pitale in his *Life of Jagannath Shankar Shett* (in Marathi), Bombay, 1916, p.70.
14. Colebrooke, op.cit., I, pp.242, 285-86 etc.
15. V.N. Datta, "Mountstuart Elphinstone: His Training, Method and Intellectual System", in Kunwar Mohammad Ashraf Commemoration Volume, Nr.63 Berin, p.181.
16. Ibid., pp.183-84.
17. Ibid.
18. Colebrooke, op.cit., II, pp. 356-57.
19. Ibid., p.357.
20. Ibid., I, p.259; II, pp. 126-28.
21. Ibid., II, p.127.
22. Ibid.
23. Choksey, op.cit., p. 271, fn. 3.
24. Colebrooke, op.cit., II, p.128.
25. Ibid., I, p.259.
26. Choksey, op.cit., p.272.
27. Colebrooke, op.cit., II, p.128.
28. Ibid.
29. Ibid., pp. 192-200.
30. Ibid.
31. Here taught Bal Shastri Jambhekar, Bhau Daji, Dadabhai Naoroji, M.G. Ranade, K.T. Telang, Pheroze Shah Mehta, N.M. Pramanand and Mr. Sorabjee Shahpoorjee Bengali some of whom acquired international fame as Indologists while others figured prominently in the political and social reform movements of India. The achievements of these worthies have been beautifully summed up by Sir Narayan Chandavarkar, himself a Elphinstonian, in his memorable address "Old Elphinstonian" delivered to the members of the teaching and student community of the

Elphinstone College in 1910 (*The Speeches and Writings of Sir N.G. Chandavarkar* (ed.) by L.V. Kaikini, Bombay, 1911, pp.410-16).

32. R.G. Bhandarkar was the first Dakshina Fellow. The fellowship was also awarded later on to M.G. Ranade, J.U. Yajnik, S.P. Pandit and others. For details see J.A. Richey (ed.) *Selections from Educational Records*, Part II (1840-1859), Calcutta 1922, New Delhi, Reprint, 1965, pp.165-67; N.K. Sharma, *Linguistic and Educational Aspirations under a Colonial System*, Delhi, 1976, pp.38-55.
33. *Journal of the Bombay Branch of the Royal Asiatic Society*, 1879, XLI-XLII.

11

Rudiments of Indian Art Historiography as Reflected in the Writings of Mountstuart Elphinstone

A historiographical approach to the study of India's contributions to the fields of fine arts and architecture was introduced for the first time by British administrator-historians and Orientalists of the Romantic School. Unlike the Utilitarians, the scholars of this school did not condemn the ancient civilisation of India but rather they viewed it in an advanced stage of development, Mountstuart Elphinstone represented the latter school of thought.[1]

Elphinstone's perception of the Indian art is reflected in his journals, letters and historical works which indeed form the basic source-material for tracing the beginnings of historiography of Indian art. Elphinstone had visited a number of historical places in India and was particularly impressed by the wonderful architectural achievements of Western India and the South. The richness and variety of the civilisation in these parts of India made a deep impact on him. Unlike Mill, whose sweeping statements provoked Indian historians to challenge western attacks on their culture, Elphinstone followed a very constructive approach providing thereby a proper perspective to the new generation of Indian scholars in the formidable task of reconstructing the contributions of their forbears to the development of world culture.[2]

Elphinstone makes full use of the then available source material *Asiatic Researches* (particularly the works of Sir William Jones, Mr. Paterson and H.T. Colebrooke), Ram Razs' *Essay on Hindu Architecture*, Orme's *Indostan*, Erskine's *Transactions of the Literary Society of Bombay*, Wilson edited *Mackenzie Papers*, Tod's 'Rajasthan' and the works of Daniells and Stirling.[3]

Tracing the historical growth of the Indian people Elphinstone did not find their arts of life in a rude state as viewed by other British historians. In his *History*, mention is made of Indian's fondness for gold and gems, ornaments and silk garments. Their sense of aesthetics is gathered from the ancient literary texts which speak of gardens, terraces, ponds, orchards, etc., by the men of wealth for the public benefit. References to various professions show all that is necessary "to civilised life, but not all required for high refinement".[4] Elphinstone observed:[5]

> In the arts of life the Indians were in the more advanced stage of society ... in the knowledge of the being and nature of God, they were already in possession of a light which was but faintly perceived even by the loftiest intellects in the best days of Athens.

Although agreeing with the view that isolation has given to the Indian culture an original and peculiar character, he however, regards it to be a misfortune for the Indians because they consequently developed a sense of superiority-revered only their own institutions and despised those of other races of the ancient world until a stage was reached when they became incapable of receiving improvements from without and averse to novelties even amongst themselves.[6]

Elphinstone's *History*, primarily concerned with the cultural achievements of the Hindus, does not provide any elaborate treatment of the development of Indian art, perhaps because of inadequate evidence at his disposal or probably due to the fact that this aspect of Indian culture was dealt with to a certain extent by such renowned Orientalists as William Jones and some of his distinguished contemporaries. This besides Elphinstone's idea was to make his study as comprehensive as possible so as not to leave any aspect of Indian cultural life untouched. This explains why he is so sketchy in his treatment of the fine arts of the Indians.

Dealing with Indian music he mentions different modes with reference to their expression and power of touching particular sentiment or affection, derivation of their names after the seasons and particular period of time. The melodies of the Indian *ragas* for their remarkable sweetness and plaintiveness stand distinguished from those of other countries, he opined. He provides a fairly accurate description of the musical sittings together with the accompaniments – the Indian lyre (*vina*), drums (mridangam and the fiddle)[7] – the reference seems to be to South Indian music. Elphinstone's comments on Indian paintings are limited to the wall paintings of the houses which came under his observation. He seems to be very disappointed at their lack of perspective and scant attention to light and shade. It may be pointed out that when Elphinstone wrote, not much was known about the cave paintings particularly at Bhaja, Ajanta, Ellora and Badami some of which have become the subject of so much of appreciation of the art critics. Elphinstone, however, makes passing reference to the art of illuminating manuscripts and portrait painting in India.[8]

The sculptural art of India is also dealt with briefly.[9] The reasons explained in connection with paintings happen to be pertinent with reference to sculpture also. This besides it may be pointed out that when Elphinstone wrote, neither the fundamentals of Indian art nor its features as distinguished from the Graeco-Roman art were clearly understood.

Elphinstone is therefore surprised to find that this land of polytheism could not inspire its artists to attain high excellence in sculptural art. Images in caves visited by him sometimes appeared very spirited but he is pained to see absence of grace in figures, total ignorance of anatomy, in brief, they showed complete disregard for the physical aspect of the art. It is, therefore, no wonder that he finds Indian sculptural art in a much lower stage of development.[10] Elphinstone, it appears, could not perceive the fundamental difference between the Indian and Greek art in respect of the concept as well as the forms, a very relevant aspect which was so remarkably expounded later by S.N. Dasgupta in his observation that:[11]

> In the Greek art the conception of gods mainly consisted in idealisation of forms of human beauty and did not involve any superior ideal or connote any superior meaning. In Indian art the gods are mostly human figures, they are not conceived on the pattern or types of human beauty. With the Greeks man was super-important and nature played an insignificant part and was therefore neglected. In India, however, man is regarded as a part of nature and the representation of man or gods was indispensably associated with the representation of such lovely forms of nature as could be in harmony with it. In short, the object of the Indian artist was not only to be faithful to nature, but to transcend it. This transcendence is an inevitable consequence of the fact that the objects of representation must first be ideally conceived and steeped in the emotion and inner intuition of the artist.

The whole objective of the Indian art as exposed in the above passage was to make the work both natural and spiritual. Elphinstone's impression about the sculptural art is superficial and does not stand in consonance with his view that Indians' knowledge of the Being and the nature of God, even the highest thinker of Greece could but faintly perceive. The spiritual foundation of Indian art was perhaps beyond Elphinstone's comprehension.

Elphinstone's review of Indian contributions to the field of architecture is relatively more detailed. Firstly, because he had before him Ram Raz's *Essay on Hindu Architecture*[12] and secondly, because he personally visited a number of architectural monuments particularly the caves at Karlee, Nasik and Ellora.[13] Ram Raz's work, the first serious and systematic attempt, has been hailed by Captain Harkness as "an epoch in the history of the science of architecture".[14] The work was commended by Elphinstone for its basically sound and judicious method, the principles of art as expounded in it and for its fairly satisfactory understanding of the extant works on the subject.[15] Elphinstone seems to have made a thorough study of Ram Raz's work, for the latter has brought to light for the first time a South Indian traditional *Silpa* text together with a fragment of the *Manasara* and studied the texts with the help of a Sanskrit scholar who was himself a good sculptor well acquainted with the practice of architecture and the terms used in the art. Ram Raz verified his understanding of the texts by reference to the monuments themselves and also making use of plates of neatly drawn and lithographed drawings to exemplify and to make the meaning clear.[16]

Elphinstone is highly indebted to Ram Raz for the account of structural constructions with such minute details as various mouldings, forms and proportions of pedestals, bases, shafts and the varying dimensions of columns.[17] As compared to Egyptian architecture solid pyramids were unknown to Indian architecture, he observed. Although pyramidal roofs to the halls before temples were known but these were hollow within and supported by walls or pillars. The south Indian style of temple architecture particularly the succession of storeys, each narrower than the one below it, flattened dome and its termination, i.e., high pinnacle of metal gilt or trident or other emblem particular to the god – all made a deep impression on him. The towers which are never plain are often stuck over with pinnacles and covered with ornaments of every description. The sanctuaries, the towers, spacious halls, surrounding courts, the colonnades and other religious buildings all receive Elphinstone's careful consideration.[18]

The temples with their decorative columns, richness and complexity, posts, lintels, the panels depicting plants, flowers, fruits, human and animal forms, i.e., "every species of embellishment that the most fertile fancy could devise" he found very impressive. The running patterns of plants and creepers in his opinion, display "an elegance scarcely equalled in any other part of the world".[19] Relief sculptures on the walls of the temples and the dimension of the Bhuvaneswar or Vijayanagar groups of temples drew his special attention.[20] The Indian pagodas as compared to the simple majesty and symmetry of Grecian temple or the grandeur of the mosques appeared to him less attractive, an observation which he explains as due to the lack of height in extensive structures and where height is obtained it is marred by deficiency in breadth besides defective combination between different parts of the temple structure.[21]

A critical appraisal of Indian architecture led Elphinstone to the conviction that in this art, as in most other things, the Hindus "display more richness and beauty in details than greatness in the conception of the whole".[22] But at the same time he admits that his observation is limited to the temple architecture in general and does not cover the cave temples where "boldness and grandeur of design' is undoubtedly exhibited".[23] The last observation is based on Elphinstone's visits to the Carlee (1802, 1812), Nashik (1810-15) and Ellora (1810-15) cave temples. These visits he remembered with great admiration. About the Carlee cave he writes:[24]

> It has a solemnity and a sort of gloomy magnificence which I do not recollect in any other Indian work. We went round all the caves. The sight now made us anxious about Buddha and his religion, and determined me to assist inquiries about them as much I can, by getting the whole of the inscriptions copied, and sent to some person in whose hand they may be useful.

Much of the interest in the record of his excursions consists, as rightly pointed out by Colebrooke, Elphinstone's biographer, "in the description of its romantic scenery, mixed with notes of the memorials of former civilisation, and the Buddhist remains that abound in Western India".[25] In his description of Sindoor (near Nashik) he does not fail to notice the marks of decay of the fort-town which must have been in the hands of more civilised possessors. He does not leave unnoticed a very ancient beautiful little temple left unfinished but still richly and elegantly sculptured. The temple he assigned to a period more than 700 hundred years old.[26] His recollections of the visits to Nasik caves, Ganesa Lena and Ellora are even more illuminating. The Nasik caves he perceived as a sort of gallery cut round the hill half way up. The caves were about fifteen or twenty, most of them quadrangular, like the secondary caves at Carlee or Kaneri. The finest was nineteen paces long and eleven broad. He describes it as follows:[27]

> There are doors opening into cells all round, except in the middle of the side fronting the entrance, where there are four handsome pillars forming the verandah to a chapel, in which sits a black figure above the human size. He sits on a chair or bench, and is somewhat tremendous, notwithstanding his gilt whiskers and white eyes.

The Ganesha Lena (a *Chaitya* hall at Junnar) was found inferior in style than those at Nasik. The largest was rectangular surrounded by cells, more open and more light without any varandah or deep chapel as was the case at Nasik, but instead it had a recess closed with a gilt grating, behind which sat Ganesha. Elphinstone did not know whether he was the original proprietor or an intruder, but two or three of the other caves were evidently designed for Buddha.[28] While on his way to Ellora, Elphinstone visited the fortress of Daulatabad which he ranked among the "strongest fortresses in the world". Elphinstone provides a vivid description of the fort, citadel, enclosed rampart, ruins of palaces and remains of gardens, ponds, ditch cut in the solid rock and takes particular note of the 'boldness in design' of the fort complex.[29]

The Kailasa temple of Ellora considered as one of the architectural wonders of the world, received particular appreciation and admiration of Elphinstone. This moment so vividly described by his biographer, is reproduced below.[30]

> Its vast and massive piles, hoary and venerable with age, yet retaining the richness and variety of the earliest days, struck me with wonder and admiration. The number of pinnacles, portals, galleries, and statues, and the profusion of ornament that was lavished on each of them seemed infinite; but what delighted me most was the view up the left of the temple as you enter. A colonnade of a great many pillars supports a mass of solid work, a hundred feet high, which projects near thirty feet beyond the pillars, forming a broken and irregular roof, and hanging over with a boldness that inspires awe and almost terror. I saw many other caves mostly belonging to Buddha. The figures, which are like those of Elephanta, pleased me, in some, the borders and ornaments in others; but the echo in the Carpenter cave (where the voice in a particular situation sounds like thunder), the magical effect of the landscape from the depth of the cave called Dannalla, were what struck me the most.

The striking originality of the architectural monuments suggests that sound principles of art were well established in India from early times.[31] Elphinstone doubts and rightly so, the great antiquity which is claimed for them. On the basis of the inscriptional evidence which the cave temples provide, their antiquity could be traced to a period sometime before the Christian era. The Hindu temples, according to him, could be placed, on the basis of the subjects depicted on their walls, sometime between eighth to thirteenth centuries.[32] These temples in no way could be assigned to a date earlier than the limits thus suggested.

Palaces, private houses, and those of the rich showed little planning or systematic arrangement and could hardly be included under the head 'architecture'.[33] Construction of magnificent tanks and wells next drew Elphinstone's attention.[34] He classifies the tanks into two categories, reservoirs for water formed digging out of the earth or by damming up the mouth of a valley. The former have steps down to the water and in many cases temples round the edge and little shrines down the steps. In the latter case these things are confined to the embankment. The lakes are generally located near towns and meant to serve two-fold purpose, bathing and irrigation. The dams were built to serve only the latter purpose. The lakes with their vast extent and magnificent embankment in respect of their elevation and solidity received special appreciation. Older wells were found square having great depth and considerable breadth while those of later times were round surrounding galleries of a rich and massey style and the steps down to the water were their common features. The bridges in the south were composed of stone posts several of which were connected by stone beams. In early times building of arches, vaults or domes was perhaps not known.[35] Erection of gateways to commemorate some victory was known. The Chittor column or the triumphal arches at Barnagar in Gujarat, Elphinstone considers among the "richest specimens of Hindu art".[36]

Among other arts, Elphinstone makes passing references to the weaving of cotton cloth which, from the point of view of beauty, delicacy and fineness of texture, had no parallel in the contemporary world. The silk manufacture was excellent, for the art of obtaining the material was known from very early times in India. The art of dyeing was also known.[37] The goldsmith's work was excellent but the art of jewellery did not attend high standard for the setting was comparatively crude.[38] Elphinstone was deeply impressed by the simplicity of Indian workmanship.

He remarks:[39]

> A smith brings his small anvil, and the peculiar sort of bellows which he uses, to the house where he is wanted. A carpenter does so with more ease, working on the floor, and securing any object with his toes as easily as with his hands.

These brief observations of Mountstuart Elphinstone, forming as it were the rudiments of Indian art historiography, need not be compared with the masterly works of Burgess, Fergusson, Havell and Smith – his distinguished successors and specialists on various aspects of Indian art. Elphinstone's approach to the study of the cultural growth of India widely differed from many scholars of the succeeding generation. He had travelled extensively, was acquainted with local conditions and had a sympathetic understanding of the Indians. Deeply interested in Indian literature, customs and traditions he visited a number of historical monuments. A real history of India cannot be written without direct contact with the Indian situation, he believed. He was full of admiration for the antiquity and vitality of the Hindu civilisation. Ancient Indian institutions, according to him, were in an advanced stage of development and that the artistic achievements though 'in a simple state' yet 'far from being rude'. Elphinstone did not study Indian culture by 'western standard' but evaluated it in the context of its 'conditioning circumstances'. And as very aptly remarked by Cowell, the charm of the style of his writings is "the spirit of genuine and hearty sympathy with, and appreciation of, the native character, which runs through the whole, and the absence of which is one of the main blemishes of Mr. Mill's eloquent work".[40]

The foregoing survey of Elphinstone's reflections on Indian art is primarily intended to provide to the inquisitive, an insight into his training, method and intellectual system. His brief observations, hampered as they are, by the inadequacy of his source-material, succeeded at least (as could be gathered from the commendable works of his worthy successors) in drawing the attention of the western scholars to the remarkable contributions of Indians to the fields of fine arts and architecture. These reflections thus become indispensable for any comprehensive view of the beginnings of the historiography of Indian art.

Notes

1. James Mill, *The History of India*, H.H. Wilson (ed.), London, 1858; Mountstuart Elphinstone, *History of India: the Hindu and Muhammadan Periods*, with notes and additions by E.B. Cowell, London, 1915; T.E. Colebrooke, *Life of Honourable Mountstuart Elphinstone*, 2 Vols., London, 1884; J.S. Cotton, *Mountstuart Elphinstone*, Oxford, 1892, Rulers of India Series; C.H. Philips (ed.), *Historians of India, Pakistan and Ceylon*, Oxford, 1961.
2. H.A. Phadke, "Mountstuart Elphinstone and the Growth of Indological Consciousness in Western India", *Proceedings*, Indian History Congress, Dharward, 1987 (Summaries).
3. Elphinstone, *History*, pp.156-63.
4. *Ibid.*, p.47.
5. *Ibid.*, p.48.
6. *Ibid.*
7. *Ibid.*, pp.156-57.
8. *Ibid.*, p.157.
9. *Ibid.*
10. *Ibid.*
11. S.N. Dasgupta, *Fundamentals of Indian Art*, Bharatiya Vidya Bhavan, Bombay, 1960, pp.12-37.
12. Ram Raz, *Essays on the Architecture of the Hindus*, posthumously published by the Royal Asiatic Society, London, 1834. Only a few details about Ram Raz are known. He was a Native Judge and Magistrate and was well-known for his learning and talent (see *infra*, fn.14 and 16).
13. T.E. Colebrooke, *Life*, I, pp.242, 280, 285-86.
14. Pramod Chandra (ed.), *Studies in Indian Temple Architecture*, American Institute of Indian Studies, 1975, p.1, Harkness' preface to Ram Raz's work, p.x.
15. Elphinstone, *History*, p.158.
16. Pramod Chandra, *op.cit.*, pp.1-2.
17. Elphinstone, *History*, *op.cit.*

18. *Ibid.*, pp.158-59.
19. *Ibid.*, p.159; Orme, *Indostan*, I, p.182 as quoted by Elphinstone with reference to Seringam temples.
20. Elphinstone, *History, op.cit.*, p.160; Stirling, *Asiatic Researches*, Vol.XV, p.307.
21. *Ibid.*
22. *Ibid.*
23. *Ibid.*
24. T.E. Colebrooke, *Life*, I, p.242.
25. *Ibid.*, p.278.
26. *Ibid.*, J.S.Cotton, *op.cit.*, p.83.
27. *Ibid.*, p.280.
28. *Ibid.*, pp.281-82. It may be pointed out that in Mahayana Buddhism a new pantheon of gods was admitted which included such Brahmanical gods as Ganesha, Shiva and Vishnu, all made subordinate to Buddha (D.D. Kosambi, *The Culture and Civilization of Ancient India in Historical Outline*, New Delhi, 1981, p.179).
29. *Ibid.*, pp.284-85.
30. *Ibid.*, pp.285-86.
31. Elphinstone, *History*, p.160.
32. *Ibid.*, pp.160-61; Erskine, *Transactions of the Literary Society of Bombay*; Wilson (ed.) *Mackenzie Papers*, Preface, p.1xx-xxi; Stirling, *Asiatic Researches*, Vol.XV, pp.315, 327.
33. Elphinstone, *History*, p.161.
34. *Ibid.*, pp.161-62.
35. *Ibid.*, p.162.
36. *Ibid.*
37. *Ibid.*, pp.162-63.
38. *Ibid.*
39. *Ibid.*, p.163.
40. Colebrooke, *Life*, II, p.357.

12

Acharya Jambhekar (1812-1846): The Pioneer Oriental Scholar and Reformer of Western India

The introduction of English system of education in the first quarter of the nineteenth century was an event of great significance in the social, cultural and academic life of Western India. It induced the newly educated people to undertake a critical study of their cultural heritage in order to remove its deep-rooted inequities and falsehoods. Among such pioneers was Acharya Bal Shastri Jambhekar who may be rightly compared with his counterpart, Raja Ram Mohan Roy, the father of renascent Bengal.

As a student Jambhekar was influenced by Sadashiv Kashinath Chhatre; the Secretary to the Native Book and School Society, and A.B. Orlebar, professor of mathematics at the Elphinstone Institute. His brilliance was noted by his teachers right from his early school days. Recognition came to him when he was appointed Deputy Secretary (1830) and Secretary to the Bombay Native Education Society (1832) before his appointment as the first Indian professor of mathematics at the Elphinstone Institute in 1834.[1] "The first outstanding star of the Elphinstone College" he delivered lectures on history and philosophy as ably as he could lecture on mathematics besides as rightly mentioned in the Report of the Board of Education "his remarkable facility and elegance in English composition gave him the reputation of an able English scholar".[2] His achievements in mathematics and astronomy were remarkably far advanced than any of his countrymen in Western India. As a linguist he was well conversant with a number of languages – Sanskrit, Gujarati, Kannada, Telugu, Hindi, Persian, Arabic, French, Latin and Greek besides Marathi which was his mother tongue. He held prominent positions in the field of education as Superintendent to the Government School (1842) and Director of the Normal Class (1832). What was remarkable of him was his ardent anxiety and zeal for the improvement of his countrymen for he firmly believed that the promotion of education and diffusion of knowledge were the initial steps for the reform of the Indian society. It was with this aim in view Jambhekar founded the Native General Library and Native Improvement Society in 1845. In recognition of his services in education and reforms, the government appointed him *Justice of Peace* in 1840.[3]

Since newspapers are the most effective means for educating public mind Bal Shastri decided to start in 1832 *Darpana* – a bilingual weekly, and then in 1840, *Digdarshana* – a monthly. *Darpana* clearly shows his acquaintance with the Bengali language and press, for it is well known that *Samachardarpana* which was founded in 1818 by Serampore Missionaries was the first attempt at Anglo-vernacular journalism in Bengal. The object of the *Darpana* as stated by its learned editor was "to encourage amongst the countrymen the pursuit of English literature and to open a field for free and public discussion on points connected with the prosperity of this country, and the happiness of its inhabitants".[4] The importance of the paper was also recognised by the *Oriental Christian Spectator* while commenting "Darpana is a highly respectable and useful paper in Marathi and English. Both its original and selected articles are well fitted to inform, expand and correct the native mind".[5] The *Digdarshana* contained original and select articles on geography, history, natural philosophy, chemistry and general science with a view to improving the mind, imparting useful knowledge to the Indians.[6]

In his editorials Bal Shastri used to enter into serious discussions on a variety of topics connected with our social system. He was in close touch with the reform movements of Bengal and was well informed about those outside India. Like his great contemporary Raja Ram Mohan Roy, he makes a fervent appeal to his countrymen to do away with the cruel and inhuman social rite of the *Sati*. He also advances arguments against another evil custom of the female infanticide. Not only did he plead for the education of women, but also for the re-marriage of the Hindu widows as far back as the thirties of the 19th century, and is said to have inspired Gangadhar Shastri Phadke for writing a book on the last mentioned subject.[7] His own contributions were, of course, three important articles which he wrote while reviewing the earliest books on the subject.[8] Bal Shastri expresses his desire that such books need to be reprinted and properly circulated among the educated pundits. The object of the aforesaid books was to establish three propositions:

(i) that female education should be encouraged;
(ii) that woman losing their husbands before the age of puberty should marry again and,
(iii) girls should marry at an early age.

In his reviews, Bal Shastri firmly asserts that marriage should be celebrated only when a girl attains the age of womanhood. He opines that the girls should not be married until they become 12 years of age although by doing this a man may not obtain virtue deserved for the giving of his daughter, he may have that which is derived from her happiness.[9] Looking at the then social conditions of Maharashtra and the fact that it was not till 1891 when the Age of Consent Act was finally passed by the government of Lord Lansdown, it must be admitted that Bal Shastri indeed took a very bold stand.

The achievements of Bal Shastri in the field of social reforms have been properly evaluated by Narayan Chandavarkar in his Presidential Address to the Bombay Provincial Social Conference of 1901.[10] While reviewing the progress of the social reforms before Justice Ranade, Narayan makes a glowing reference to the work done by Bal Shastri Jambhekar. Bal Shastri persuaded Jagannath Shankar Seth to espouse the cause of the young man named Shripad Sheshadri, who was a convert to Christianity but desired to enter again into the Hindu fold. There was a great deal of insurrection in the orthodox society of Maharashtra, who opposed tooth and nail to the readmission of the young man to Hinduism. The opposition was led by Dhakji Dadaji, who was considered to be the prominent member of the Hindus of Bombay. But Bal Shastri, in spite of the fact that he had to suffer excommunication for five long years, made tremendous efforts and ultimately succeeded in getting round the community in admitting the young man to the Hindu society. The credit for making the first breach in the stronghold of the orthodox Hindu society goes obviously and rightly so to Acharya Jambhekar.[11]

In a letter to his brother-in-law dated November 19, 1843, Bal Shastri directs attention to the nefarious activities of the Christian missionaries in forcibly converting poor and innocent Hindus to their faith.[12] He sincerely believed that readmission of such persons to the Hindu society is all the more necessary for the preservation and existence of the Hindu religion, and expressed his desire to educate public opinion in favour of such a movement. Bal Shastri was thus the forerunner of the Shuddhi Movement which was started later on by Arya Samaj under the direction of its founder Dayananda Sarasvati.

Himself devoted to the best teachings and practices of the Hindu faith and believing in the ancient saying, *svadharme nidhanam shreyah*, he was singularly free from the prejudices of caste, creed or sect. Not only did he preach but himself lived a life of moral purity, religious toleration and universal brotherhood. Bal Shastri held to the opinion that reform in society is no more possible without religion and the best way to break down caste distinctions is to begin slowly purifying the religious practices of the people. His deep knowledge of Hindu scriptures made him alive to the hollowness of many of religious rites and social customs. A great admirer of the western education he believed that it would free Indians from the shackles of superstitions. Once in a public lecture he explained the true causes of the eclipse and called as useless all religious rites which are performed on such occasions. For this he was again threatened with excommunication by the orthodox section of the society but Bal Shastri, a man of great courage as he was, could not be bowed down by such moves and continued to follow the dictates of his own conscience and convictions in matters of social reforms. A great social force of his time, Bal Shastri is thus considered to be the initiator of three important movements of Maharashtra: Widow remarriage, *shuddhi* and the publication of newspapers.[13]

Bal Shastri was not unmindful of yet another feature of the renaissance namely, the growing interest of researchers, both Western and Indian, in the study of the antiquities and the ancient literature of India. In Western India the beginning was made by Sir James Mackintosh in the foundation of the Literary Society of Bombay in 1804, while the legislative and educational reforms of Mountstuart Elphinstone initiated measures for the promotion of Oriental researches in the Bombay Presidency. The Bombay Literary Society merged itself into the Royal Asiatic Society as its Bombay Branch in 1829 and later on John Wilson, the distinguished Orientalist became its President in 1835. While expounding the objects of the society Wilson asked its members to investigate into the various aspects of Indian life "physical, historical, literary, religious and administrative". The earliest representative of this Indological consciousness was, as remarked by Wilson "the distinguished Bal Shastri Jambhekar, one of the most learned natives of Western India". Bal Shastri wrote several papers on antiquities of India, to the Journal of the Bombay Branch of the Royal Asiatic Society. It is recorded of him that when the doors of the Society were not opened to the Indian members, Bal Shastri had only to send his papers through the Secretary of that body. Nevertheless, he was appointed Secretary to the Translation Committee of the Society to procure translations from the original languages into European languages. He was also elected to the membership of the Bombay Geographical Society and contributed largely to its transactions.[14] He was something of a genius, as skilled a modern scholar as he was an erudite Shastri.

His papers on copper-plates and rock inscriptions bearing on the early history of India appeared in the earliest numbers of the Society's journal and as very aptly put by Chandavarkar "he was the first antiquarian scholar among the Hindus who enriched the literature of this Society". Bal Shastri's contributions consisted of publication of facsimile of ancient inscriptions some of which he brought to light for the first time, with Devanagari transcript and English translations. It shows that he was well conversant with the reading of the Brahmi script. These inscriptions he copied from various places – Palitana, Girnar, Kharepatan, Nagpur, Kolhapur and Samangarh. The Kharepatan and Samangarh grants are related to the Rashtrakuta dynasty of the Deccan while the Note on a specimen of iron ore in the vicinity of 'Malwa' is of a technical nature. His research papers have left a distinct mark of the depth and vastness of his scholarship.[15]

Bal Shastri was a prolific writer. His major works include *Theory of Equations, Elements of Differential and Integral Calculus, Sarasamgraha or Catechism on General Knowledge, Abridgement of Murrary's English Grammar, Rudiments of Geography, Etymology of the Marathi Language,* (jointly with Vinayak Divekar and Bhau Mahajan). *History of England* (2 vols.), *History of British India* and the *History of India.* He edited and brought out the lithograph edition of the *Jnaneshvari* besides a number of useful articles on a variety of subjects –

chemistry, physics, geography, astronomy, psychology, history and palaeography published in the *Digdarshan* to make the readers aware of the technological and scientific advancement through the ages.[16] His works on history although in the form of translations and abridgements of the original English works nevertheless show his deep interest in that discipline which he considered essential for a proper understanding of the contemporary times. The inspiration perhaps came from the writings of Elphinstone who wrote the earliest satisfactory history of ancient and medieval India. Elphinstone underlines social change, provides details and offers explanation, and free from preconceived notions, he admires the antiquity and vitality of Hindu civilisation in some of its features.[17] It was Bal Shastri who first published an abridgement of this work in Marathi.

Wilson in reply to Morebhat Dandekar's *Hindu Dharma Sthapana* wrote a book under the title *An Exposure of the Hindu Religion*. Appreciating the stand taken by the latter scholar Bal Shastri wrote in his editorial:[18]

> We believe Morebhutt's is the first instance of a Brahman coming forward publically to vindicate the Hindu religion, and entering the field of public discussion by publishing a work in defence of it.

As a perceptive critic of other's work Jambhekar's merit, can be judged from his review of Vans Kennedy's *Researches into the Nature and Affinity of Ancient and Hindu Mythology*.[19] Although not agreeing with all the conclusions of Kennedy, Bal Shastri points out that the learned scholar did not impose his own conceptions regarding the Hindu religion but has represented it according to the Shastras. Bal Shastri is full of appreciation for Kennedy who unlike Bentley and other western scholars did not assign sacred books of the Hindus to the last seven or eight hundred years but traced them back to at least a period of three thousand years, also pointing out numerous striking coincidences between the ancient world and Hindu mythology. And the close affinity between Sanskrit and most of the ancient languages as shown by Kennedy in an earlier work led Jambhekar to the suggestion that probably most of the ancient religious systems had their derivation from the Hindu mythology. Kennedy's cursory remarks on the impact of Hinduism on the human mind also contents much truth and candour Bal Shastri contends.[20]

The move of several western scholars like Trevelyan, J. Prinsep, Tytler, A. Duff, and H.T. Prinsep to bring about the "Romanization of the Indian Alphabets" was strongly opposed by Bal Shastri through an editorial in the *Bombay Darpan*.[21] The proposal was adopted in the Bengal Presidency. After a careful consideration of every argument advanced in favour of such a proposal Bal Shastri was convinced that the substitution would not serve any useful purpose. He pointed out that the notions of western scholars regarding the phonetic values of Indian alphabets were erroneous and that the translations of ancient texts in Roman characters would defeat the very purpose of imparting knowledge to the native of India and further, for the "convenience of a handful of Europeans", such a suicidal course in academic matter need not be adopted. Bal Shastri very ably combatted the view of Sir William Jones in alleging a belief on the part of the Hindus regarding the theory of divine origin in reference to the Devanagari alphabet. He further showed that the letters of the alphabets, that is their sounds, are in artificial order in which they are arranged in Panini's Vyakarana. The sound of speech are nearly the same in every language and therefore, nothing is gained by the substitution as far as they are concerned.[22] Concluding his arguments, Bal Shastri remarked:[23]

> As to the forms by which sounds are expressed, no Hindu ever adduces a divine origin for them; in fact, they are not the same as those in use in time of antiquity, which after receiving successive modifications have at last assumed

> their present form. In either point of view, therefore, it cannot be maintained that, by the substitution of the new alphabet, the natives are weaned from a superstitious conceit, since the conceit has no real foundation.

John Wilson too agreed with the views of Jambhekar whom he regarded "the most capable of judging in the case in this part of the country at least".[24]

The premature death of Acharya Jambhekar in 1946, a man of such a brilliant career and many sided activities naturally came as a great shock to the cause of rational and intelligent social reforms and oriental researches depriving the historian of forming an estimate of what he had been had he lived longer. Paying tributes to his remarkable achievements A.B. Orlebar, the editor of the Journal of the Bombay Branch of the Royal Asiatic Society, wrote:[25]

> In the death of the late Bal Gangadhar Shastri, remarkable among the native community for grand talent and acquirements, the Society has lost, a valuable and most useful contributor of inscriptions, that branch to which Lassen has particularly called the attention of our members as being the only means of obtaining a clear and authentic knowledge of the early history of our country.

And, Erskine Perry, while assessing the place of Acharya Jambhekar among the great Indians of the early nineteenth century, observed:[26]

> To the wide range of information and the enlightened morality resulting from an excellent European education, to the most solid and rare attainments in science and literature, both European and Asiatic, and to the influence which was the just and natural result of a character and mind thus distinguished and adorned, he added an anxiety and zeal for Native improvement which I have never seen

equalled; and which have forcibly impressed upon my mind the conviction, that the loss of no individual in Bombay, European or Native of whatever rank, could prove so great a calamity to Western India, as of our lamented friend, the late Bal Shastri.

Notes

1. S.F. Sen (ed.), *Dictionary of National Biography*, Calcutta, 1974, Vol.II, pp.229-30; for detailed biographical material see G.G. Jambhekar, *Memoirs and Writings of Acharya Bal Shastri Jambhekar* (1812-1846), 3 Vols (in Marathi), Poona, 1950.
2. Report of the Board of Education for the year 1846.
3. S.P. Sen, *op.cit.*
4. *The Bombay Durpun*, January 6, 1832, Prospectus; G.G. Jambhekar, *op.cit.*, Vol.II, p.1.
5. *The Oriental Christian Spectator*, March 1833.
6. *The Digdurshun*, Vol.I, No.1, Introductory; G.G. Jambekar, *op.cit.*, Vol.II, Section III, pp.1-3.
7. P. Padhye and S.R. Tikekar, *Ajakalacha Maharashtra*, Bombay, 1935, p.78.
8. *The Bombay Durpun*, August 13, September 8 and 15, 1837.
9. *Ibid.*
10. Narayan Chandavarkar, *Speeches and Writings*, Bombay, 1911, pp.93-94.
11. *Ibid.*, see also his address "On Old Elphinstonians", pp.413-14.
12. G.G. Jambhekar, *op.cit.*, Vol.III, Appendix II, Some Important Letters and Papers, pp.495-97.
13. Padhye and Tikekar, *op.cit.*, p.79.
14. J.J. Modi, *Centenary Memorial Volume of the Bombay Branch of the Royal Asiatic Society*, 1905; *Index to the Transactions of the Literary Society of Bombay*, 1885; *Transactions of the Bombay Geographical Society*, Vol.III.
15. For Jambhekar's contributions to epigraphy see *JBBRAS*, Vol. I, Nos. II, III, V, VII; Vol.II, Nos. VIII, X, XI.
16. G.G. Jambhekar, *op.cit.*, Vol. I, pp.62-64, 66-68.
17. V.N. Datta, *Mountstuart Elphinstone: His Training, Method and Intellectual System*, pp.176-86, *Kunwar Mohammad Ashraf Commemoration Volume*, Akademic Berlin, Nr.63.
18. *The Bombay Durpun*, April 13, 1832.

19. *Ibid.*, February 3, 1832.
20. *Ibid.*
21. *The Bombay Durpun*, February 5, 1936; *The Oriental Christian Spectator*, March, 1836; G.G. Jambhekar, *op.cit.*, Vol.III, pp.616-20; *The Application of the Roman Alphabets to all the Oriental Languages* by Messers. Trevelyan, J. Prinsep, Tytler, A. Duff and H.T. Prinsep, Serampore Press, 1834, Vol.8.
22. G.G. Jambhekar, *op.cit.*, Vol. III, pp.616-17; 619.
23. *Ibid.*, p.619.
24. *Ibid.*
25. A.B. Orlebar (ed.), *Journal of the Bombay Branch of the Royal Asiatic Society*, Vol.II, (July 1844-1847), Preface.
26. G.G. Jambhekar, *op.cit.*, Vol.I, p.24-5.

13

Social Studies in Western India during the Nineteenth Century

Historiography of the Indian social order has drawn considerable attention of scholars in recent times. The School of Oriental and African Studies, University of London, organised a series of study conferences (1956-58) to survey and evaluate the course and character of historical writings on the people of Asia.[1] In the proceedings of one of these conferences, R.S. Sharma presented a very interesting paper entitled "Historiography of the Ancient Indian Social Order" wherein he observes:

> Problems of Ancient Indian society have been largely studied, especially by Indians, against the background of the necessity for social reform.[2]

In the light of this important statement, an attempt would be made in the following pages, to examine the nature of the social studies in Western India during the nineteenth century.

It is not that social problems were not discussed in a rational spirit before. In the Upanishadic texts, in the dialogues of Mahavira and Buddha, in the edicts of Ashoka, in the classical works of Bhasa, Kalidasa and Bana, in the commentaries of Medhatithi on Manu and some of the Shakta texts like Mahanirvanatantra this is amply reflected. Universal love, tolerance, brotherhood are all indeed very noble ideas but one has to understand them in the context of Indian social evolution. The very fact that a great reformer like Buddha failed to act positively by not imposing upon his followers the duty of neglecting their caste in social relations and that Ashoka, the medieval Bhakti saints and the nineteenth century religious and social reformers had to stress time and again on tolerance and promotion of peaceful coexistence among various religious and social groups, bespeak of the social, cultural and religious constrains all through the ages.[3] There is, therefore, some justification for R.G. Bhandarkar's lamentation that "India had no social and political revolutions" though she did experience 'religious revolution'.[4] The earlier reform movements did not look upon the caste system as a social evil (as was conceived by the reformers of modern times) and hence they remained content with some change in the religious and moral spheres. Even the radical thinkers like the Ajivikas and the Lokayatas although they vehemently attacked Brahmanical concept of karma, rituals and *varna* system, they did not provide any positive answer to the social problems of the day. Unfortunately so little is known about the social views of these philosophers that we cannot say with any amount of certainty "whether they remained true to the principal of rational radicalism not only in thought but also with regard to the social questions".[5]

Nevertheless, it may be pointed out, that the social questions continued to draw the attention of scholars on Dharmashastra literature who glorified the old system of family and *varna* in their determined bid to stem the tide of social change which was being felt especially at lower levels, due to the powerful impact of the Bhakti saints of the Sultanate and later periods of Indian history. The Indian social life, it must be admitted, was moulded by religious ideals particularly the three pursuits of life (*Dharma, Artha and Kama*), and by the concerted efforts of ancient lawgivers for making law an integral part of religion and ethics.[6] It is, therefore, no wonder that Kamalakara Bhatta, a noted Sanskrit scholar of Varanasi who flourished in the early seventeenth century was inspired to write a book on the position of the Shudras, exposing the traditional view on the basis of about one hundred and seventy-five works of which many are heard for the first time?[7] It may be that many of the works became extinct during the period of turmoil when our centres of learning were put under constant threat of attack and destruction at the hands of foreign invaders. As a large number of authorities are quoted by Kamalakara Bhatta it may be presumed that their works were also available at the time when he wrote his treatise. That so many works were composed on the subject during earlier periods, shows the extent of the degraded position to which the Shudras were reduced and the attempts made by the traditional writers to stress time and again the legal sanction against them, and how limited must be the impact of the reformers of the Bhakti school.

The Bhatta family originally hailed from Paithan in Maharashtra, a region which was profoundly influenced by the teachings of Bhakti saints during the medieval times. With the only exception of Ramadasa, there was hardly any leader associated with that movement who had shown any awareness of the maladies, the contemporary society was suffering from, or suggested any remedies, through his writings or actions, to remove them.[8] They may be called at the most reformists whose objective was not to bring any change in the existing social order. The great saint Jnaneshvara, for instance, whose family suffered so much at the hands of the orthodox section of the society, favoured upholding and preserving traditional values, not to talk of effecting any change in the prevailing social structure.[9]

It was only after the establishment of the British rule when Mounstuart Elphinstone took over as the first Governor of the Bombay Presidency that Western India began to show signs of coming change. Elphinstone considered growth of scientific spirit among the Indians as indispensable for their moral regeneration. This formed the very basis of his proposed reforms in the social, educational and legal systems of western India.[10] He preferred disassociation of education from religion and stressed the need of cooperation between state and private efforts and a system of grant-in-aid. "It will be better to lose the country by the efforts of our liberality than keep it like Dutch men or Spaniards",[11] he believed. Elphinstone's constructive suggestions in favour of the abolition of the evil social customs like the burning of the widows, infanticide, slavery, and for the continuation of the village panchayats, reflected his anxiety for and urgent need of the reform of Indian social and judicial system.[12] It is no wonder that Elphinstone's such benevolent reform measures succeeded in inducing new generation of educated Indians to undertake a critical study of their heritage in order to remove their social inequities and falsehoods.

It would be interesting to note that most of the early social writings in western India were the products of the Brahmin class, particularly those belonging primarily to the teaching community or of legal profession (Jambhekar and Bhandarkar are classical examples of the first category, while Ranade, Mandlik, Telang and Chandawarkar admirably represent the second one). This besides, a Brahmin rule was overthrown and there was an urgent need to pacify that community which was the chief beneficiary under the previous educational system.[13] Elphinstone was therefore, in favour of giving protection to this community.[14]

Among such pioneers who were deeply impressed by Elphinstone's reform measures, mention may be made of Acharya Jambhekar (1912-1846), the first Indian professor of mathematics, who started in 1832 *Darpana*, a bilingual weekly and then in 1840 *Digdarshana*, a monthly "to open field for free and public discussion on points connected with the prosperity of this country" and the happiness of its individuals, and as put by the *Christian Spectator* "to inform, expand and correct the native mind".[15]

Bal Shastri's ideas on the social problems of the day are gathered primarily from his editorials and some of his personal letters.[16] He closely followed the reform movement of Bengal started under the leadership of Ram Mohan Roy. He was a crusader against such social evils as Sati, female infanticide and was a staunch advocate of women education and remarriage of the widows.[17] His contributions on these subjects have come down to us in the form of review articles[18] wherein Bal Shastri is seen asserting firmly that marriage should be performed when a girl attends the age of womanhood.[19] It was considered during those early days a very courageous stand specially when we remember that it was only in 1891 that the Age of Consent Act was finally passed.[20] N.G. Chandavarkar, while reviewing the progress of social reforms in western India, made complimentary reference to the tremendous efforts of Bal Shastri in readmitting Shripad Sheshadri, a Christian convert, to the Hindu fold.[21/22] This was achieved despite the toughest opposition of the orthodox section of the Hindu society. Bal Shastri was deadly opposed to any forcible conversion and was keen to educate the masses in favour of a movement which could readmit such persons to their original fold.[23] Bal Shastri thus paved the way for the later Suddhi Movement of the Arya Samaj.[24] He was above caste and sectarian prejudices and advocated universal brotherhood and religious toleration. An admirer of the western education he hoped it would free the Indian mind of all superstitious beliefs and practices. In a public address he explained to the people the true causes of eclipse and exposed the unsoundness of the religious rites performed on that occasion. He was fully aware of the correlation and interdependence of the reforms in the social and religious beliefs and practices of the people.[25] Bal Shastri, in view of his multidimensional reform activities is hailed, and rightly so, the initiator of three distinct trends in the socio-intellectual life of Western India, namely, widow-remarriage, Suddhi and Anglo-vernacular journalism.[26]

The cause of social reform was pursued by yet another pioneer, Vishnu Shastri Pandit (1827-76) who concerned himself mainly with the problem of the marriage of the Hindu widows of which he was, in fact, the earliest and most strenuous supporter. He also took active part in reforming the old customs and beliefs of the Hindu society, an objective which he could successfully carry out through the Marathi newspaper *Induprakash* of which he was the proprietor and editor. During the period 1861-63, he also edited the Marathi monthly *Pune Pathasalapatrika* and held discourses, kirtans and meetings on the subject of reform. Associated with the department of education in various ways, Vishnu Shastri produced a number of valuable books on many social issues of his time like the widow-remarriage, interpretation and relevance of the Smritis, the rights of women, the duties of a Shudra, validity of foreign travel and dinning with the Shudra and the social responsibility of providing for the performance of the last rites of the orphans and other neglected classes. His critical study of the ancient texts together with a proper understanding of the modern western scientific view convinced him that reform in social and religious aspects of life was the prerequisite for India's growth into a nation. He was very much anxious to see historical sense develop among the educated. His Marathi translation of Murray's *History of India* was considered by M.G. Ranade, the reviewer, as "one of the compositions which possessed literary merit". He sincerely believed that the Indian scholars should devote their attention to things and persons near home and furnish the natives with the history of their own country and that of their rulers, rather than that of the 'Esquimaux', a race whose history can be advantageously and with propriety be put off.[27]

Vishnu Shastri's writings on social problems of the day stand in close comparison to that of Pandit Ishvarchandra Vidyasagara. Vishnu Shastri's *Induprakash* was named after *Somaprakash* of Vidyasagara. This perhaps earned him the popular title 'Ishvarchandra of Maharashtra'. Through his paper Vishnu Shastri brought out the Marathi versions of Vidyasagara's original Bangla and Sanskrit writings, for the benefit of his readers from western India. In 1866 Pandit started a reform society named 'Punarvivahottejaka Mandali' and carried on an intensive propaganda under its banner to win public support for widow-marriage. While expressing his views on the subject, in a letter to the editor *Times of India* (November 9, 1868), he succeeded in establishing on rational grounds, that such a practice was an established institution in former times and that there is absolutely nothing wrong if it comes into vogue in the present. In support of Vidyasagara's views on the subject he published *Vidhavodvahaviveka* with an English introduction. As Secretary of the Remarriage Society he took great pains in arranging the remarriage of a Brahmin widow on April 15, 1869. It was celebrated with great pomp and show and was attended by such celebrities as Wilson, Hunter, Mackperson, Bhau Daji, V.N. Mandlik, M.G. Ranade, R.G. Bhandarkar, Dhirajlala Mathuradas and many others.[28] Vishnu Shastri's social reform measures were appreciated by European scholars at Bombay and Poona while eminent orientalist G. Buhler, in one of his letters, made the following complimentary remark about Pandit's work:[29]

> Dear Mr. Vishnu Shastri, you know how I interest myself for your fight about the remarriage of widows and that, for my part, am convinced that it was frequently practised in Ancient India.

Vishnu Shastri's impact on the social life of Western India is quite discernible from the tributes paid to his memory by the Anglo-vernacular Press and by such luminaries as M.G. Ranade, R.G. Bhandarkar, V.N. Mandlik and G.H. Deshmukh[30] who were themselves distinguished for contributions to the intellectual and moral regeneration of the people of the Bombay Presidency. The *Times of India* (10.5.1876) commenting on Vishnu Shastri's lifework wrote:[31]

> The Pandit knew and felt that reform could not be revolutionary, and that it must tread in the old footsteps, that the future must grow out of the past, that there must be a legitimate basis in the Shastras, to which one must appeal if he desires to take the people with him, that in a community which was once great and pure, and which has been degraded by priestly pride and perversion into ignorance, helplessness, and corruption, such a legitimate basis can be found for all desirable reforms in the old revered books of revelation and their authorized interpretations, and that, therefore, there was no occasion to cut up the past by its roots and engraft the stocks on the future from foreign civilisations. In this belief he worked and hoped and suffered, and if success be accepted as the test and justification of the correctness of his views, it cannot be denied that success to his efforts to an extent not vouchsafed to those who are working in the cause of reform without securing a foothold on the past.

Vishnu Shastri thus anticipated the social philosophy of Ranade and Bhandarkar when he advocated reforms in all walks of Indian life and like them sincerely desired that the educated should not allow the western influence to prevail upon their minds at the sacrifice of their own cultural heritage. He was thus against any headlong actions in social matters. Such were the ideas of this pioneer social reformer of western India who worked ceaselessly, in a true missionary spirit, to win public support for the cause he represented.

The work of Jambhekar and Pandit was extended to new dimensions by the writers of the succeeding generation. The Orientalists, trained in western research methodology, concerned themselves with the formidable task of critically editing the Dharmashastra and Smriti texts along with all available commentaries composed during the succeeding periods. Among such scholars was Rao Bahadur V.N. Mandlik (1833-89) whose edition of the *Manavadharmashastra* (1886) with the commentaries of Medhatithi, Sarvajnanarayana, Kulluka, Raghavananda, Nandana and Rama Chandra[32], received high appreciation of the renowned Indologists Max Mueller and Monier Williams, Whitney, Jolly, Kielhorn, Buhler, Weber and of such learned bodies as the Royal Asiatic Society of Great Britain and Ireland and the University of Lyden.[33] The work is considered as one of the primary sources for any serious research into the social history of the Indian people. This besides, his other scholarly works were, the critical editions of *Vyavaharamayukha* and *Yajnavalkyasmriti* and the *Hindu Dharmashastra* (in Marathi, 1865).[34] His editions of the Mayukha and the Yajnavalkya Smriti were reviewed by Justice K.T. Telang in the *Indian Antiquary* (February, 1882) who considered them as an outcome of meticulous work providing detailed information on the sources of Hindu Law, and containing elaborate discussion, in a series of appendices, on special topics with reference to the decisions of British Tribunals.[35]

To what extent Mandlik was persuaded in his scholarly works by his views on social and religious reforms, it would be difficult to say. Possibly his considerations were purely academic. His personal views on all these matters can be gathered from the news magazine *The Native Opinion* of which he was the editor till 1871. As a man of strong religious convictions, Mandlik remained mostly a traditionalist in matters of reforms. He favoured women's education but was opposed to co-education. He was for equal status to women and abolition of dowry but considered widow-remarriage as derogatory to the Hindu society and yet he was a member of the Society for Encouragement of Remarriage. Furthermore, he believed in child-marriage, was against state interference in social matters and resented the religious activities of the Christian missionaries.[36] It must be admitted that Mandlik was basically a moderate traditionalist but was not against reform measures to the extent that these do not offend the popular feelings or break the traditional values of the Hindu society.

This scholarly tradition was continued by R.G. Bhandarkar (1837-1925) who produced a number of brilliant essays on social problems, namely, the caste system, age of marriage and position of women, history of widow-remarriage, the social history of India (contributed to C.Y. Chintamani's *Indian Social Reform*)[37] besides his learned addresses to various social conferences and reform associations[38], all based on a critical comparative study of the primary sources, in fact, provided the desired ideological background to the social reform movement of Western India. It may, further be noted that passages for translation incorporated in Bhandarkar's Sanskrit Readers, clearly reveal his anxiety to draw attention of students even at primary stages of education, to the social maladies prevailing in India through the ages.[39]

Most of Bhandarkar's writings are outside the scope of the present study which is limited to the nineteenth century. But here only a few comments be made. Bhandarkar lamented that India had 'no social, and political revolution' though she did experience 'religious revolutions' and felt that the absence of strong political and national feelings have resulted in the perpetuation of a system based on caste restrictions. The condition of Indian women was another pressing problem which drew the attention of Bhandarkar. He condemned the practice of female infanticide, polygamy and polyandry and considered early marriages as positive obstacle to the healthy development of the Indian society. He believed that the seclusion of women was an inheritance of later times, and Muslim domination had contributed to its rigidity. Bhandarkar was greatly disturbed at the depressed condition and illiteracy of the lower classes. The chronic poverty of our peasants who were "everywhere a prey to the rapacity of the money lenders" was a matter of serious concern to him. He suggested establishment of an Agricultural Bank to provide loans to the peasants at lower rates of interest and regretted the apathy of the government in such matters. Bhandarkar was not an advocate of headlong action in social matters. He explained how the motive forces of reform be tempered in a manner not to lead us to cut ourselves off from a living connection with the past. The social reform movement should be based on the principles of reason, truth and justice, he firmly believed.[39a]

Towards the last quarter of the 19th century, the social question did not remain confined to academics alone but became a matter of public concern and was adopted for discussion in the proceedings of various social associations and reform conferences. The interdependence of our social, religious, economic and political systems came to be well recognised. Justice Ranade (1842-1901) regarded it as "not merely an accident of history" but as the law of our nature. With a prophetic vision he declared:[40]

> You cannot have a good social system when you find yourself low in the scale of political rights, nor can you be fit to exercise political rights and privileges unless your social system is based on reason and justice. You cannot have a good economical system when your social arrangements are imperfect. If your religious ideals are low and grovelling you cannot succeed in social, economical and political spheres.

Ranade's religious views were influenced by the pure monotheism of the Upanishadas. He had highest regard for Indian saints and exhorted the people to follow their teachings. Ranade was among the foremost reformers of Western India. He denounced the caste-system and untouchability, supported widow-remarriage and was all for the enhancement of the status of women. He gave free expression to his views on all such matters in the *Induprakash* of Bombay and the *Quarterly Journal of the Sarvajanik Sabha*, Poona, of which he was the editor for sometime. The fundamental idea of Ranade's social philosophy was that we should introduce reform in such a way that no violence was done to the ancient customs and traditions. "We could not break with the past if we would; and we must not break with it if we could", he concluded.[41]

Yet another name which figures in matters of reforms is that of K.T. Telang (1850-1893), a younger contemporary of Mandlik and Ranade. Pherozeshah Mehta regarded him as "an authority on all matters concerning Hindu social reform and legislations on it". His address "Should social reform precede political reform?" was intended as a rejoinder to Sir Auckland Colvin, Lt. Governor of the United Provinces, for his advice to Indians to set their own house in order in social matters. Telang pleaded that social reform and political reform could go hand in hand, reflecting thereby the type of the role which he himself desired to play in Indian public life.[42]

In the domain of social reform Telang ranked very high. In one of his memorable address he pointed out that "Modern Civilisation did not bring with it peace but a sword to fight for justice". But like Vidyasagara, Pandit, Agarkar and Phule, he was never known for any radical steps in matters of social reform. After giving tough fight to the orthodox section of the society in the controversy over the Age of the Consent Bill of 1891, he had the marriages of his two daughters performed at the ages of nine and thirteen. For this he had to face severe criticism and condemnation even of his friends and admirers.[43]

But it is in the fields of educational and judicial reforms that Telang is more remembered. His ideas on education reveal his broad vision and progressive outlook. To him, the problem of women education was of highest concern. As a President of the Hindu Union Club whose objective was to promote "social union by interchange of ideas and sympathies", he succeeded admirably in bringing together the elite among the Hindus of all castes and sections. This besides, he was known more for his profoundly scholarly activities. His exhaustive notes on Age of Consent Bill and his rich contributions to the Proceedings of the Student's Literary and Scientific Society and the *Indian Antiquary*, were sufficient to establish his reputation as an Indologist of a world class. In fine, he was "the noblest type of a Hindu and, therefore, of an Indian exemplified".[44]

Among other writers of the nineteenth century whose attention was drawn towards the social reforms were G.H. Deshmukh, Jyotiba Phule, N.M. Paramananda and G.G. Agarkar.

Gopal Hari Deshmukh (1823-1892) was better known as *Lokahitavadi* (i.e., champion of the peoples cause) the pseudonym under which he used to write for the Poona newspaper *Prabhakara*. He also edited *Hitechchhu*, a weekly in Gujarati and was closely associated with the leading newspapers *Induprakash* and *Jnanaprakash* from Bombay and Poona respectively. It was mainly through the press that he entered into serious discussion of the social problems of the day, namely, child marriage, widow-remarriage, degraded position of women, burning of the widows, infanticide, caste distinctions, the role of the orthodox section in the decline of the society, prohibition, traditional approach to religion, untouchability and slavery of any form. These issues were throughly analysed and discussed by Lokahitavadi in a series of articles in the *Prabhakara* during 1848-50, which, later appeared as a separate volume entitled *Shatapatren* (A Hundred Letters).[45] In these letters, he treated subjects which hitherto had not been touched upon by the vernacular press and thus introduced 'new concepts and turn of phrase'.[46] He was one of the earliest advocates of 'Swadeshi' in Western India and was associated with the Arya Samaj and the Theosophical Society of which he was also the President. He was critical of the Brahmins for arresting the progress of the society by fostering anti-social tradition and was bold enough to point out that many a social custom and religious belief had no relevance to the modern times.[47] He analysed the reasons for India's loss of independence which he put down to observance of old feudal practices and the gap separating the nobility and the Indian people.[48] In his call for the spread of enlightenment, Deshmukh with a remarkable foresight, predicted that it would take the Indians at least two hundred years to free themselves from British tutelage.[49]

Jyotiba Phule (1827-1890) was perhaps the earliest reformer of western India from among the lower classes whose cause he vigorously pursued through the 'Satyashodhaka Samaj' founded by him (1873). His own literary works on the subject were *Sarvajanik Satyadharma Pustaka* and *Gulamagiri* while his newspaper *Dinabandhu* was dedicated to the exposition of the priestly class for its role in the decline of Indian society.[50] Jyotiba's contributions to the social studies have come down to us in the form of his public addresses and writings through the press. Real progress of the country he believed was not possible without proper education of the women and of the lower classes. In various ways he did devote his life to the cause he stood for, may it be founding of a girls school or a library for the lower classes (1848) or night school for adults or farmers (1855) or an orphanage for widows (1866) specially for those from the orthodox section who went astray or fighting for the rights and social justice for the lower classes through the Samaj whose doors were open to all castes even to the Jews and the Muslims. His evidence before the Hunter Commission (1882) shows his solicitude for education of the women and of the lower classes. Through his 'Samaj' Jyotiba tried to reform the marriage rituals by dispensing with the Brahmin priest making it a simple affair and won the case in the Bombay High Court on this issue. In religious matters he was an atheist. He was against the practice of Sati and the tonsure of widows. He encouraged widow-remarriage but opposed early marriage which he considered as the greatest obstacle in the way of female education. He favoured western system of education but at the village level he suggested, it should consist of Modi and Balabodha scripts, accounts, general history, geography, grammar and elementary agriculture. He declared that the Congress could not be truly national until its leaders showed genuine interest in the welfare of the lower classes. His writings received popular recognition because these were primarily aimed at exposing the degraded position of the women and lower classes in the Hindu society.[51]

Phule's social philosophy, although it displayed his genuine anxiety and deep concern for the uplift of the women and the depressed classes, lacked proper historical perspective and hence, failed to receive immediate recognition, yet his life-long work of complete devotion and immense sacrifice remained a source of inspiration for most of the writers on social themes of the succeeding generation.

Narayan Mahadev alias Mama Paramananda (1838-1893), an Elphinstonian and an associate of M.G. Ranade, K.T. Telang and Malabari, was yet another social thinker and reformer of the later half of the nineteenth century to reckon with. He was profoundly influenced by Huelings and had a close friendship with William Wedderburn. The life and work of Benjamin Franklin and aims and objectives of the Prarthana Samaj were other contributory factors which shaped Paramananda's life. From 1860 to 1863 he worked as a teacher in government schools and then in 1863 took up the editorship of the Marathi newspaper *Induprakash* and in 1864 joined the *Native Opinion* on a three years contract basis during which tenure he did the commendable task of exposing irresponsible and corrupt British officers like Arthur Crawford, Principal Kirkham and Mr. Russell. He was closely associated with the establishment of Prarthana Samaj in Bombay (1867) which was working almost on the same lines as Brahmo Samaj of Bengal. In 1873, he also took over as the editor of the *Subodhapatrika*, an organ of the Prarthana Samaj. He was a great champion of the cause of widow-remarriage and social, political and economic equality of women. He fought bitterly in the 'Dadaji versus Rakhamabai case' (1884-87) to vindicate the woman's right to refuse to stay with her husband if he suffered from a serious malady or vices.

He denounced caste and untouchability and advocated true and compulsory primary education for all.[52]

Building of the free, just and enlightened social order in India was the mission of his life. In his advocacy of social reform he primarily used the medium of journalism so as to reach every class of educated Indians. His journalistic achievements, known mainly through his writings in the *Induprakash*, the *Native Opinion* and the *Subodhapatrika*, are remarkable for their thought content and his revolutionary ideas on social change. Being a government servant, Mama did not participate in political movements yet he was called 'Political Rishi' by no less a person than M.G. Ranade because of his vision, foresight and clear perception of the Indian conditions. Himself living a simple and quiet life, Mama was essentially a social worker who performed his self assigned task with great dedication, courage and perfection.[53]

The last of these social thinkers was Gopal Ganesh Agarkar (1856-95), a younger contemporary of Phule and Paramananda. His indepth study of Indian social problems are known mainly through his contributions to the *Kesari* (1881-87) and *Sudharaka* (1888-95) of which he was the editor. His writings were remarkable for the originality of ideas, clarity of imagination, emotional appeal and poetic tenderness. Influenced by the philosophy of Spencer and Mill he critically examined Indian social system on the basis of pure reason. He denounced caste and untouchability as unnatural and degrading restrictions on the individual. Although the amazing proliferation in the Hindu society of every form of conceivable inequality came under Agarkar's severe attack, yet he was not quite happy with even the flexible clan structure of the West based on income and wealth. He fought for raising the marriage age of boys to 20-22 years and for girls to 15-16 years. He was a strong supporter of widow-remarriage and associated himself openly with such marriage ceremonies. He deplored the lower status of Hindu women and was never tired of exposing even the smallest disability of which they were victims. He was an advocate of compulsory education for boys and girls and believed that the position of widows could be well improved by teaching them some useful occupation. He approved western system of education as the 'agency of social progress and equality of opportunity'. The causes of India's bondage are to be sought in Indian circumstances, in our lack of certain basic qualities which could be acquired only by reforming our political and social system, he believed, Hindu-Muslim unity Agarkar considered as a prerequisite for Indian liberation and severely criticised the policy of divide and rule of the British administration.[54]

The beginnings of the social studies in western India during the 19th century can thus he traced to the progressive measures of administrators like Elphinstone who considered improvement in the education system as essential for the moral regeneration of the Indians and that administrative structure should aim at the reform of Indian social and judicial systems. This enlightened policy made profound impact on the intellectual life of western India. The Elphinstone Institute which was founded in 1834, in course of time, developed into a nucleus of a great intellectual movement. Many of the outstanding social thinkers selected for the study, were, in fact, educated at this centre of learning and it was here that they taught and prepared the younger generation of scholars for the formidable task of revitalisation of the Indian society. Jambhekar, Ranade, Mandlik, Bhandarkar, Telang and Paramananda belonged to the Elphinstonian school of thought while Pandit, Phule and Agarkar were the best representatives of the Poona reformist school. It is true that except Bhandarkar, and to a certain extent Ranade, none of them could be designated as social historian (most of them took to journalism), yet their perception and analysis of the social maladies which were at the very root of our national decline, provided the conceptual framework so very necessary for any serious inquiry into the historical growth of the Indian social order.

Concluding Remarks

Our reflections on the genesis and growth of the intellectual and social movements of Western India during the nineteenth century now come to a close. They began with Mountstuart Elphinstone's rational policy in matters of social, judicial and educational reforms and Bal Shastri Jambhekar the Elphinstonian, applied it to the fields of journalism, oriental studies, and such social problems as the widow-remarriage and readmission of the converts to the original faith. R.G. Bhandarkar addressed the academic community on sense of duty, love of truth, and love of justice; M.G. Ranade exposed the interdependence of our systems social, religious, economic and political, while V.N. Mandlik and K.T. Telang represented the judicial view and along with Bhandarkar and Ranade they preferred historical method while interpreting Indian tradition. V.S. Pandit, G.H. Deshmukh and Jyotiba Phule championed the cause of Indian women and the downtrodden sections of the society, while, N.M. Paramananda and G.G. Agarkar studied these problems purely from a rational angle for which they chose journalism as their chief medium.

As a result of these strenuous efforts, the Indians, in course of time, became mentally prepared to demand their legitimate share in the governance of their own country. This is what Elphinstone predicted in his memorable report on education.

It may be asked as to why some outstanding names like B.G. Tilak, S.M. Paranjape and V.K. Rajawade have not been included in this study. It is true that these names have a permanent claim to the remembrance of modern Maharashtra. Tilak for his dominating role in the Indian freedom struggle besides providing new dimension to Indian spiritual thought, that too from his imposed seclusion of the prison cell; Paranjape for introducing a revolutionary trend in Indian journalism and Rajawade for his original and remarkable contributions to the history of the Marathas and other writings with his strong nationalist fervour, all this, it may be pointed out, is mostly spread over the early twentieth century and therefore, remains beyond the scope of the present inquiry. This important aspect, however, needs to be taken up in a separate study.

To conclude, the intellectual and social movements of Maharashtra as discussed above, provide the necessary backdrop for the regeneration of the Indian people during the twentieth century.

Notes

1. C.H. Philips (ed.), *Historians of India, Pakistan and Ceylon, Oxford*, 1961.
2. *Ibid.*, p.107.
3. H.A. Phadke, "National Integration: The Historical and Philosophical View", Indian National Trust for Art and Cultural Heritage, *Newsletter*, December, 1991, p.14.
4. R.G. Bhandarkar, *Collected Works*, Poona, II, pp.478-79.
5. K. Antonova, G.Bongard Levin, G. Kotovsky, *A History of India*, Moscow, 1979, I, pp.113-14; 154.
6. R.S. Sharma, *op.cit.*, pp.112-13 for a brief reference to the scholars, both foreign as well as Indian, representing the idealist viewpoint.
7. Kamalakara Bhatta, *Shudrakamalakara Athava Shudradharmatatva Prakasha*, Bombay, Nirnayasagara, V.S. 1936.
8. P. Padhye and S.R. Tikekar, *Ajakalacha Maharashtra*, Bombay, 1935, p.25ff; V.K. Rajawade, *Sri Samartha Ramadasa*, Ananda, Satara, Saka, 1848, pp.15-29; V.L. Bhave, *Maharashtra Sarasvata*, pp.313-35 for a detailed study of Ramadasa and his work.
9. Bhave, *op.cit.*, pp.113-14.
10. Sir T.E. Colebrooke, *Life of Honourable Mountstuart Elphinstone*, 2 Vols., London, 1884, II, p.151ff; Elphinstone's Minute, December 13, 1823.
11. Colebrooke, *op.cit.*, II, pp.156-62.
12. *Ibid.*, p.154; R.D. Choksey, *Mountstuart Elphinstone (The Indian Years 1796-1827)*, Popular Prakashan, Bombay, 1971, pp.144-37.
13. Choksey, *op.cit.*, p.386.
14. *Ibid.*; H.A. Phadke, "Mountstuart Elphinstone and the Growth of Indological Consciousness in Western India", Indian History Congress, Dharwad, 1988, *Proceedings*, Summary, p. 168.
15. H.A. Phadke, *Acharya Jambhekar (1812-1846): The Pioneer Oriental Scholar and Reformer of Western India, Ratna Chandrika*, (ed.) Devendra

Handa and Ashvini Agrawal, New Delhi, 1989, pp.395-402; *The Oriental Christian Spectator*, March, 1833.

16. *Ibid.*; G.G. Jambhekar, *Memoirs and Writings of Acharya Bal Shastri Jambhekar*, Poona, 1950; Padhye and Tikekar, *op.cit.*, p.78.
17. H.A. Phadke, *op.cit.*; *The Bombay Durpan*, August 13, September 8 and 15, 1837.
18. *Ibid.*
19. *Ibid.*
20. *Ibid.*
21. Narayan Chandavarkar, *Speeches and Writings*, Bombay, 1911, pp.93-4.
22. *Ibid.*; See also his address "On Old Elphinstonians" pp.413-14.
23. G.G. Jambhekar, *op.cit.*, III, Appendix II, "Some Important Letters and Papers", pp.495-97.
24. H.A. Phadke, *op.cit.*
25. *Ibid.*
26. Padhye and Tikekar, *op.cit.*, p.79.
27. S.S. Pandit, *Vishnu Parashuram Shastri Pandit Yanche Charitra*, Poona,1936, pp.6-12, 13-17, 77-90; Padhye and Tikekar, *op.cit.*, pp.120-21, *Dictionary of National Biography*, (ed.), S.P. Sen, Calcutta, 1974, III, C.B. Khairmoday's brief note on Pandit, pp.300-301.
28. S.S. Pandit, *op.cit.*, pp.13-48; *DNB, op.cit.*, The widow-remarriage was sanctioned by the Act of 1856.
29. S.S. Pandit, *op.cit.*, p.36; *DNB, op.cit.*
30. S.S. Pandit, *op.cit.*, pp.99-128.
31. *Ibid.*, pp.102-103.
32. G.R. Havaldar, *Rao Sahib Vishvanatha Narayana Mandlik Yanche Charitra*, Vol.II, Bombay, 1927, pp.827-33.
33. *Ibid.*, pp.832-33.
34. *Ibid.*, I, pp.334-35.
35. V.N. Naik (ed.), *Select Writings and Speeches of K.T. Telang*, Vol.II, pp.385-404.
36. *DNB*, III, 1974, A.R. Kulkarni's note, pp.40-41.
37. R.G. Bhandarkar, *Collected Works*, II, pp.538-83 (Age of Consent Bill, 1891); pp.443-70 (*Social History of India*); pp.471-86. (*The Indian Caste System*, 1915); pp.458-69 (Position and Influence of Women in Indian Society, 1901; ZDMG, XLVII (*History of Child Marriage*, 1891) pp.143-53; H.A. Phadke, *R.G. Bhandarkar*, National Book Trust, India, 1968, pp. 61-68.
38. R.G. Bhandarkar, Presidential Addresses: "The Ends and Aims of College Education", 25th Anniversary, Deccan College, Poona, 1868; "Social Reform and the Programme of the Madras Hindu Social Reform Association", Madras, 1894; Indian Social Reform Conference, 1895;

Bombay Provincial Social Conference, 1902, Sholapur; H.A. Phadke, *op.cit.*

39. *Second Book of Sanskrit*, 27th edition, Bombay 1988, pp.151, 161.

39.a H.A. Phadke, *op.cit.*, pp.61-75.

Bhandarkar's observations on the growth of Indian society come somewhat closer to those of Rammohan Roy, R.C. Dutt, Swami Dayananda, John Muir and Weber where they display a marked tendency to quote ancient scriptures in support of modern reforms. His well documented pamphlet on the Age of Consent Bill amply corroborates it. This viewpoint has been very well summed up by Bhandarkar himself in the following words:

In ancient times girls were married after
they had attained maturity, now they must
be married before; widow-marriage was in
practice, now it has gone out ....
Interdining among the castes was not prohibited,
now the numberless castes cannot
have inter-communication of that nature.

(*Collected Works*, II, pp.522-23; see also R.S. Sharma, *op.cit.*, pp.102-07.)

40. C.Y. Chintamani (ed.), *Indian Social Reform*, pp.27-8.
41. *Ibid.*; N.R. Phatak's note on Ranade in *DNB*, IV, 1974, pp.332-341; V.N. NAIK, *op.cit.*, Vol. I and II.
42. N.S. Karnataki's *Biography of Telang* (in Marathi), Bombay, 1929 for detailed study.
43. *Ibid.*
44. *DNB, op.cit.,* IV.
45. K.N. Athalye, *Lokahitavadi Hyanche Charitra,* Poona, 1926; N.R. Phatak, *Arvachina Maharashtratila Saha Thora Purusha*, Poona,1949; and *DNB*, 1972, I, pp.435-36 for his brief note on Lokahitavadi; Padhye and Tikekar, *op.cit.*, pp.81-99; G.H. Kelkar, *Lokahitavadi,* Poona, 1937.
46. *Antenova*, Levin, Kotovsky, *op.cit.*, II, pp.79.
47. *DNB*, V, 1972, pp.435-36 for N.R. Phatak's brief note.
48. *Antonova*, Levin, Kotovsky, *op.cit.*, p.69.
49. *Ibid.*
50. *DNB*, III, pp.354-56 for V.G. Hatalkar's note; for details see Phule's works: *Gulamgiri* (Poona,1873), *Jatibhedavivekasara* (Bombay,1865), *Ishara* (*A Warning*, Poona, 1885) and *Sarvajanika Satyadharma Pustaka* (Poona,1889) and also Padhye and Tikekar, *op.cit.*, pp.100-109.
51. *Ibid.*
52. P.B. Kulkarni, *Mama Paramananda Ani Tyancha Kalakhanda*, Bombay, 1963; D.G. Vaidya, *Prarthana Samajacha Itihasa; DNB*, III, pp.309-10.

53. *Ibid.*
54. *DNB*, I, pp.19-20 for S.K. Muranjan's brief biographical note; for detailed study see: *Sudharaka*, 1893; V.N. Naik, *Biography of G.G. Agarkar*, Bombay, 1916; M.D. Altekar, *G.G. Agarkar: Charitratmaka Nibandha*, Bombay, 1930; Iravati Karve, *Agarkar Darshana*, Poona,1956; D.N. Shikhare, *Principal G.G. Agarkar*, Poona,1950; V.S. Khandekar, *Agarkar: Vyakti Ani Vichara*, Poona, 1951; Padhye and Tikekar, *op.cit.*, pp.160-79.

Appendix

MEN AND MATTER
As Gleaned from the Original Sources

On the Effects of New Education
Lecture, September 4, 1823

"We are educating the natives. Here it is even more important and more hazardous experiment.... it will be better for us to lose the country by the effects of our liberality than keep it like Dutchmen or Spaniards, not that I think the immediate danger of our losing the country increased by education... but there can be no doubt that when the natives get more extended nations they will expect, first a share of their own government and then the whole."

Life of Honourable Mountstuart Elphinstone, T.E. Colebooke, London, 1884, II, pp.157-60; *Mountstuart Elphinstone*, B.D. Choksey, Bombay, 1971, pp.396-97.

On the Indian Arts of Life

"In the arts of life the Indians were in the most advanced stage of society...in the knowledge of the Being and nature of God, they were already in possession of a light which was but faintly perceived even by the loftiest intellects in the best days of Athens."

Mountstuart Elphinstone, *History of India: The Hindu and Muhammadan Periods*, London, 1915, p.48.

Objectives of the Darpana (6 January, 1832)

"To encourage amongst the countrymen the pursuit of English literature and to open a field for free and public discussion on points connected with the prosperity of this country, and the happiness of its inhabitants."

(Balshastri Jambhekar)
Biography (in Marathi), G.G. Jambhekar, Vol. II, p. 1.

A Convocation Address (1894)

".....we are living in a momentous period in the history of India. Upon our conduct at this period depends the future of our country.... The intellectual and moral sense of the country must now wake up... thought on every subject of interest to humanity must be stimulated. The great inequities and false-hoods of our social institutions and customs must be corrected...and religion purified and refined.... In this process of regeneration the ideas or principles which alone will guide us safely are sense of duty, love of truth and love of Justice."

R.G. Bhandarkar, Vice Chancellor, University of Bombay, Collected works, Vol., pp.450-51.

The Systemic Interdependence

"You cannot have a good social system when you find yourself low in the scale of political rights, nor can you be fit to exercise political rights and privileges unless your social system is based on reason and justice. You cannot have a good economical system when your social arrangements are imperfect. If your religious ideals are low and grovelling you cannot succeed in social, economical and political spheres. It is not merely an accident of history but the law of our nature".

Justice Ranade [C.Y. Chintamani (ed.) Indian Social Reform, pp.27-28]

विधवा विवाह (जाहिरात) 1864

विधवा-विवाह धर्मशास्त्रास पूर्ण संमत आहे. आज पावेतो विधवा-विवाह करण्यास शास्त्रीय, लौकिक अथवा युक्ति-प्रयुक्तीच्या जितक्या म्हणून हरकती निघालेल्या लोकांच्या ऐकीवात आहेत

त्यांचे धर्मशास्त्राधारे उत्तम रीतीने खंडन केले आहे.
अविभक्त हिन्दू कुटुंबातील बायकांची स्थिती शुद्ध गुलामाप्रमाणे असते. तिला उपमाच मिळणे कठीण. सत्यदीपिका, 1867.

Widow-remarriage is allowed by the Dharmashastras and that the position of women in the Hindu undivided family is comparable to that of the slaves.

(V.S. Pandit)

Biography of V.S. Pandit (in Marathi), S.S. Pandit, Pune, 1936, pp. 24, 126.

सवयी आणि अभ्यास

कोणत्याही देशाच्या मोठेपणाची इमारत सत्य व उद्योग या दोन मजबूत चिन्यांवर उभारावी लागते. या दोहोंसही अभ्यासाची जोड लागते. हिन्दुस्थानातील लोकास धीरत्वाची (ही) आवश्यकता आहे.

Patience, love of truth and industry are the basic requirements of the Indian people.

'नेटिव्ह ओपिनियनची' उद्दिष्टयें

राजकीय, सामाजिक व नैतिक विषयांवर नेटिव्हांची स्वतंत्र मते प्रसिद्ध करावचायी.

To publish the independent views of Indians on political, social and moral subjects, is the aim of '*The Native Opinion*'.

धार्मिक स्वातंत्र्य

आमची अशी समजूत आहे की कोणी कोणाच्या धर्मांत हात घालू नये. तर ज्या सरकारचा अवतार आमच्या धार्मिक स्वातंत्र्याचे पालन करण्याकरिता आहे, त्याने तर आमच्या धर्मांत ढवळा-ढवळ शेवट पर्यंत करू नये. भगवद्गीतेत सांगितले आहे की, मनुष्य जर आप आपलीच कामे करीत राहील तर त्याला सिद्धि प्राप्त होईल (स्वे स्वे कर्मण्यभिरत: संसिद्धिं लभते नर:). मिलचे सारे ग्रंथ वाचून जेवढे ज्ञान होते, त्याच्याहून आमच्या सामाजिक इतिहासाचे ज्ञान या एका चरणाच्या वाचनाने होते.

The government should not interfere in the religious practices of the people. The Bhagvadgita advices men to follow faithfully the work assigned to them. This course would lead to their supreme attainment.

स्त्रीस्वातंत्र्य

तेथील (इंग्रजांतील) प्रकार विशेषत: स्त्री जातीला प्राप्त झालेले स्वातंत्र्य व वरिष्ठ दर्जाही पाहून मी चकीत झालो. आमच्या देशात स्त्री-पुरूषास ही स्थिती केव्हा प्राप्त होईल?

The social equality and freedom enjoyed by the English men and women should be the aspiration of the Indian people.

(V.N. Mandlik)

Life and Works, (ed.) G.R. Havaldar (in Marathi), Bombay, 1927, Vol.I, pp.130, 151, 195, 271, 285.

शास्त्र व रूढी

(हिन्दू यूनियन क्लब, व्याख्यान, 1886)

माइयामते मूळ शास्त्रकारांचा हेतू असा असावा की, देश, काल, वर्तमान याकडे लक्ष देवून धर्मशास्त्र नियमांत वेळोवेळी शिष्यांनी विचार करून फेरफार करावे. असे केल्याने स्मृतिकारांचा शहाणपणा व दूरदर्शीपणा दिसून येतो. जे धर्म नियम एका स्थितीत सोईवार असतात, ते स्थित्यंतर झाल्यावर प्रतिबंधक होवून असुखास कारणीभूत होतात.

जुन्याकडे आमचा कल असला पहिजे, हे म्हणणे मला मान्य आहे. पण तेजसेच्या तसे आम्ही राखणार हे म्हणणे व्यर्थ आहे. आपल्या देशात पुनर्विवाहीची पद्धत होती याला दाखले मिळतात. तरी हे कबूल केले पाहिजे, आणि हल्लीच्या परिस्थितीमध्ये विवाह करू इच्छिणान्या विधवांना आडकाठी असता कामा नये. कालमानाप्रमाणे पूर्व विचार करून सत्य स्मरून जी सुधारणा करावयाची ती आमची आम्हीच करणे चांगले.

The basic concepts of our legal authorities seem to suggest progressive changes in our social and legal systems according to time and space. We need not follow our old beliefs and practices literally. We must change our customs voluntarily as required by our own times. There are evidences to show that the practice of widow-remarriage was in vogue in ancient times.

सामाजिक विषयासंबंधी तडजोड

(व्याख्यान, 1889)

आपली ईश्वरासंबंधाने, समाजसंबंधाने व राष्ट्रसंबंधाने काय कर्तव्य कर्मे आहेत या बद्दल प्रत्येक सुशिक्षित मनुष्याने आपल्या बुद्धीप्रमाणे खोल विचार करून आपली मते होईल तितक्या अंशाने कायम केली पाहिजेत आणि असे ठरविताना 'न हि सत्यात्परो धर्मः' हेच महावाक्य प्रमाणभूत मानले पाहिजे.

Every educated Indian should be allowed to formulate his duties on spiritual, social and national concerns according to this own conscience. While doing so he should not get away from the truth which in fact, is the supreme Dharma.

(Justice Telang)

Biography of Telang (in Marathi), N.S. Karnataki, Bombay, 1929, p. 112.

मानवी हक्काची सनद व विश्वधर्म
(शतपत्रें, क्र. 64)

सर्वांनी ईश्वराचे भजन अन्तकरणापासून करीत जावे; जसा आपला जीव तसा दुसऱ्याचा मानावा; जे करावचाये, ते स्वभाषेत अर्थ समजेल असे करावे; प्रत्येकास आपले विचाराप्रमाणे आचार करण्याची व बोलण्या लिहिण्याची मोकळीक असावी; स्त्री-पुरूषांचे अधिकार धर्मसंबंधी कामात व संसारात एकसारखे असावे; आचारापेक्षा नीति प्रमुख असावी, आचारांचे महत्व हल्ली आहे तसे असू नये; मनुष्यमात्रास तुच्छ मानू नये; जाति अभिमान नसावा, सर्वांनीसारखे दयापूर्वक वर्तावे, सर्वांचे कल्याण करावे; स्वदेशाची प्रीति, त्यांचे कल्याण विशेष करून मनात वागवावे; सरकारकडून प्रजेचे अधिकार अधिक असावे म्हणजे जे जे रेयतेच्या हिताचे कायदे आहेत ते सरकारशी भांडून घेत जावे. विद्यावृद्धीसाठी सर्वांनी मेहनत करावी, दु:खीतास सुख, रोग्यास औषध, मूर्खास ज्ञान व दरिद्रयास शक्त्यनुसार द्रव्य देण्यास अवमान करू नये. विद्याज्ञान संपादनास सर्व सारखे अशी मोकळीक असावी.

Faith in God, equality of all human beings, love for ones mother tongue, rejection of irrelevant social and moral code of conduct, freedom of speech and action, equality of men and women, love for ones own country and its welfare, care of the health and education of the down trodden are the basic rights of the people to be granted by the government; if, otherwise, should be acquired by continuous struggle. This constitutes the charter of Human Rights and Universal Religion.

[Lokahitavadi (G.H. Deshmukh, Shatapatren, No.64)]

मानवतावादी उदारमताचा जाहीरनामा
(गुलामगिरी; सार्वजनिक सत्यधर्म पुस्तक)

स्त्री-पुरूष हे उभयत:च स्वतंत्र आहेत. निर्माणकर्त्याने सर्व स्त्री-पुरूषास मान, धर्म व राजकीय स्वतंत्रता दिली आहे. दुसऱ्या व्यक्तीचे हक्क हिरावून घेवू नयेत.

नवरा बायको सोडून इतर स्त्री-पुरूषांनी बहीणभावाप्रमाणे आचरण करावे. आपल्या सर्वांच्या निर्माणकर्त्याने एकंदर सर्व मानवी हक्काविषयी आपले पाहिजेत तसले विचार व्यक्त करण्यास स्वतंत्रता दिली आहे. परंतु या विचारांपासून कोणत्याही व्यक्तीचे कोणत्याही तऱ्हेचे नुकसान होवू नये, अशी खबरदारी ठेवली पाहिजे. कोणत्याही धर्मसंबंधी मतावरून किंवा राजकीय मतावरून कोणास कोणत्याही प्रकारे नीच मानून त्याचा छळ करू नये. कोणीही मानव प्राणी यांची हत्या करू नये, किंवा त्यांची हत्या करण्यास मदत करू नये. कोणाही मानवप्राण्यास पिढीजात कपटाने अपवित्र वा नीच मानू नये.

Equality of men and women should be maintained. Freedom of thought and action to be granted to all. Religious and political views need not determine the status, high or low, of an individual. Untouchability to be completely abolished and the policy of non-violence to be adopted while dealing with all human beings. These are the fundamentals incorporated in the Gulamagiri or a treatise on the True and Universal Religion.

[Jyotiba Phule (S.M. Mate, Adhunika Sudharaka, pp.46-48)]

खरा सुधारक

लोकांच्या कल्याणाचा जो हेतू मनात धरला असेल तो कोणत्या उपायाने लौकर तडीस जाईल व कोणत्या साधनाने एकंदरीत आपल्याला किंवा दुसऱ्याला कमीतकमी त्रास होईल याचा शांतपणे निश्चय ठरवून तदनुसार वर्तन करावे हेच सत्पुरूषास योग्य आहे. हा निश्चय करताना खरी सुधारणा कशात आहे हे फारच काळजीने ठरविले पाहिजे. कारण, वारंवार होते काय की, विशिष्ठ वासनाधीन किंवा मताधीन झालेल्या मनुष्यास वास्तविक सुधारणा कशात आहे हे नीट न समजून जेवढे जुने असेल तेवढे फेकून देण्यात व कसल्या तरी नवीन गोष्टीचा अंगीकार करण्यात आपण सुधारणा करीत आहोत असा भ्रम होतो: ज्या देशात आपले शेकडो पूर्वज जन्मास आले, वाढले व मरण पावले, ज्या देशात हजारो पिढयांनी अनेक गोष्टीत मोठया कष्टाने केलेल्या सुधारणांचे फळ आपणास ऐतेंच प्राप्त झाले, अशा देशातील धर्माचा, रीतिरिवाजांचा व लोकांचा सर्वथैव त्याग करणाऱ्या मनुष्यास खऱ्या सुधारकाची पदवी कधीही शोभणार नाही. स्वभूमीत, स्वलोकात, स्वधर्मात आणि स्व-आचारात राहून अविचारी व अज्ञान देशबांधवांच्या निंदेस किंवा छळास न भिता, त्यांच्याशी भांडून, कधी युक्तिवाद करून, कधी लाडीगोडी लावून, अथवा सामर्थ्य असल्यास कधी त्यांना दटावून त्यांची सुधारणा करणे यातच खरी देशप्रीति, खरी बंधुता, खरा देशाभिमान, खरे शहाणपण व खरा पुरूषार्थ आहे. याच्या उलट जे वर्तन करतात ते सुधारणा करीत नाहीत, तर फक्त श्रृंखलांतर करतात! अशाच्या कपाळी लिहिलेली खरी गुलामगिरी कधीही सुटावयाची नाही.

(आगरकर: व्यक्ति आणि विचार, संचालक व प्रस्तावक वि.स. खांडेकर, पुणे 1959, पृ. 183-84, नं. 17)

A true reformer is one who is deeply concerned about the welfare of the people. Real reform does not consist in having a bias nor does it lie in rejecting all that is old and accepting all that is new. A true reformer should remain in his own country and among its people, he should be aware of their short-comings in social and religious matters and try to improve them. This needs to be done patiently, rationally and if required, even by putting pressure on them. Real patriotism, brotherhood and wisdom lie here. Those who work otherwise do not deserves to be called reformers, in fact, they are the real slaves.

[G.G. Agarkar]

Index